Full of Joy

Seeking and Finding God in Paradise

Walt Lichtenberger

Enjoy finding God in Paradise,

Walt

ISBN: 978-1-7345607-1-8

DEDICATION

To Katie, who brings joy in paradise.

CONTENTS

ACKNOWLEDGMENTS

Joy has filled my heart since I started my call at Christus Victor Lutheran Church in Naples. I am grateful for the people, the Council, and the Staff. You have welcomed me in love and revived my spirit for ministry. It is a pleasure being with you "another day in paradise."

I am also grateful for the many readers who follow my daily devotionals. Your reading what I have to offer brings me joy. Thank you for the encouraging words and comments along the way.

The stories in this book come from various folks and conversations. I am particularly thankful to Dave Marries, James Christiansen, Susan O'Brien, and the Rev. Doug Wahlberg for your extended insights.

I am deeply grateful to Connie Lange, who edited and proofread this book. You helped not only to check but also to shape it. Thank you.

Last, I would be remiss if I didn't express my appreciation to my wife, Katie. Your love and support make facing challenges and opportunities possible every day. Thank you for agreeing to follow me to paradise and for the life we share here, soaking up the sunshine.

INTRODUCTION

When I exited the airport terminal, a warm breeze welcomed me to South Florida. Palm trees shaded the path to the rental car building. It was like I had entered another world. A few hours earlier, I had watched the aircrew de-ice the plane at my upper-Midwest point of origin. Winter's snow and cold vanished behind me, yielding to the land of endless summer. As I have said many times since that moment, "It is hard to argue with sunshine."

After that visit to the Sunshine State and many intensive conversations surrounding it, I accepted a call to serve as a pastor of a congregation in Naples, Florida. For the second time in my married life, my wife Katie and I moved away from family and friends to minister in a faraway place.

Such things are challenging and bring a sense of sadness and commotion. A steep learning curve accompanies dramatic moves. Everything is new. Everything from grocery and hardware stores to medical care, licensing bureaus, insurance, housing, post offices, shopping centers, and highways is cattywampus. Confusion settles in, with second-guessing not far behind.

And yet, with the changes in latitudes come new perspectives, experiences, and opportunities unimagined. When old patterns and habits break, there is a possibility for new growth, healing, and refreshment. You begin to appreciate and view things differently.

So it was and continues to be for me as I moved over a thousand miles out of my comfort zone. Even though I am still on that proverbial learning curve, I am grateful for the welcome we received, the friendships that have formed and the old ones that have continued, and the chance to preach the gospel in such a unique setting.

From my interactions with folks from all walks of life, engagement with the nature surrounding me, and an ongoing quest for spiritual fulfillment, I have caught glimpses of God's presence, which have brought joy.

In this book, I will attempt to share the joy that fills me in the life God has given in this place called "paradise." It is not to say that what follows omits sorrow and struggle; it does not. Nor is it a commercial for the easy life in "paradise"; it is not, as true paradise was lost ages ago in Eden. I don't pretend to have the answers to make all life's problems disappear; this is not a self-help resource. I also won't guarantee that all your doubts about God and life will vanish; faith doesn't work like that, and I have yet to scrape the surface of the mystery of God.

I will say this - time spent seeking God's presence and ways is well-spent even if we can't orchestrate or anticipate the outcome of our investment. Further, whether we find ourselves in "paradise" or not, intention and focus on spiritual matters yields reward.

As we breathe mindfully, pray, study scripture, share compassion and kindness, give generously, question, and dialogue with others, we will grow in our identity as beloved children of God. The promise of finding God accompanies our active seeking of God.

When we find God, even the slightest glimpse, joy will come. It will come as the Bible describes it. Sometimes it arrives in random bits and pieces. Occasionally, it shows up as we get off the plane and head into ventures of which we cannot see the ending. But joy will come; when it does, it will fill our soul.

One who knows about such things is Archbishop Desmond Tutu, who provided moral leadership in his country of South Africa during the apartheid struggle. In a conversation on joy with the Dalai Lama, Tutu observes,

> "When you show compassion, when you show caring, when you show love to others, do things for others, in a wonderful way you have a deep joy that you can get in no other way. You can't buy it with money. You can be the richest person on Earth, but if you care only about yourself, I can bet my bottom dollar you will not be happy and joyful. But when you

are caring, compassionate, more concerned about the welfare of others than about your own, wonderfully, wonderfully, you suddenly feel a warm glow in your heart, because you have, in fact, wiped the tears from the eyes of another."[1]

Community, connection, and compassion - these three values, exemplified in Jesus's life and expressed throughout his teaching, are critical components of joy. Without them, we might experience pleasure and even happiness for a time, but we will miss the lasting joy of which the Bible speaks. Being full of joy is a spiritual experience we share with God and others.

Over centuries, human cultures, experiences, and religions have yearned to connect with God, each other, and creation. This desire is a spiritual quest involving the soul and the whole body.

People come to South Florida for various and sometimes conflicting reasons. Although there are natives who grew up here watching overdevelopment forever change the landscape of "Old Florida," many more residents came here from somewhere else. Some come for employment, while others come here to retire. Some are poor refugees who flee oppression in their homelands, while others, who are wealthy, seek shelter from taxes.

---

[1] Tutu, Desmond, the Dalai Lama, and Douglas Abrams. The Book of Joy: Lasting Happiness in a Changing World. New York, AVERY an imprint of Penguin Random House, 2016.

4

Yearly, the population swells as vacationers flock to the beaches and amusements Florida famously offers. There are many choices for fun in this place of perpetual sunshine.

Whereas it is safe to say that most do not come for spiritual reasons, nobody leaves their souls at home. Because we can't separate our souls/spirits from our bodies, the restless search for God accompanies us wherever we go. It is also as true for vacationers, "snowbirds," and year-round residents of the Sunshine State.

"Thou hast made us Thyself, and our hearts are restless till they rest in Thee."

These timeless words of St. Augustine of Hippo appear etched into a stained glass window that hangs in a window of my church study in Naples. Throughout the day, varying degrees of sunshine illuminate the window's bright colors of a Western artist's rendering of the famous bishop from North Africa.

The window once hung in Bethany Lutheran Church in North Bergen, New Jersey. It was there on the Sunday of my baptism in 1971. Donated by my Grandfather Lichtenberger in memory of my Grandmother, it was the unofficial marker of our family pew.

That's where we sat from when my mother carried me as an infant until we moved away following my Confirmation in eighth grade. The window outlasted my family's participation in the congregation's life.

Sadly, Bethany Lutheran Church closed its ministry. After a mortgage default, the bank repossessed the building and sold it to a developer, who was buying properties on the block for a new residential project. My brother convinced the developer, who was biding his time before demolishing the building, to let him have the window.

Although it meant nothing to the agents of progress, I count the window as a priceless treasure. I am grateful that my brother rescued it and gave it to me to celebrate my fiftieth birthday. The stained glass brings me joy daily.

It also reminds me of the restless search for God and the meaning of life that Augustine describes in his late fourth-century work on his conversion to Christianity. When he wrote <u>Confessions</u>, Augustine was in his late forties and a leader in the Church.

With the wisdom of retrospect, Augustine recounts the unsatisfying nature of his youthful wandering of various pleasures. Nothing fills him with lasting joy until he finds a life in Christ. Though he continues to yearn for a deep connection to God and purpose in life, Christianity provides a fruitful path for his journey. The faithful witness of other Christians, including his mother, is vital in his quest.

The quest for God is not only for African bishops of the fourth century but continues today. Whether we identify it as such or not, that feeling of emptiness in our spirits that sometimes seems insatiable is the same spiritual journey. We can't turn it off or down. We can try ignoring it and might successfully suspend it for years as Augustine did in his youth, but it will eventually resurface and intensify.

The restlessness might catch us by surprise when we least expect it. Perhaps even when we are on vacation or resting from our everyday routines. Apart from the busy rush of life, it is possible that we finally find space to recognize the inner longing for something more. Relaxed, a yearning might emerge to seek a greater connection with our Creator and our spiritual purpose in life.

Or maybe the restlessness is part of the craziness that characterizes our over-scheduled and stressed-out existence. With all that goes on, we might not recognize anything "spiritual" in the swirl of active living. Going from one thing to another, missing a couple of items along the way, it might seem like we are always on autopilot. How satisfied are we with such a life? Where do we find purpose and meaning at the end of the day? If such things are elusive, I will guess that spiritual restlessness is part of what troubles.

Since the spiritual quest to find rest in God is a constant life-long journey, regardless of where you find yourself today, whether you are chill or choking, there is a benefit in taking a reflective pause. Stop and breathe. Breathe deeply and take a moment to recognize our need for God, our purpose, and the meaning in all our relationships. Breathe as a beloved creature created by a loving God.

From our intentional breathing and centering, let us engage in the quest of seeking and finding God where we find ourselves. For some, this will be a physical place that can be identified on a map. Maybe you find yourself reading this book on a snowy day in the Upper Midwest, or a rainy day in the Pacific Northwest, or a humid day on the East Coast, or a sweltering day in the Southwest. Perhaps you find yourself in paradise.

In Southwest Florida, "paradise" is used regularly. This tropical designation is supported by plentiful palm trees, continually blooming flowers, pristine beaches, and exotic birds. The island vibe invites a laid-back attitude.

Surrounded by natural splendor and a carefree outlook, I wondered as I wrote this book, "Is this what Eden was like?" Seeing a Hibiscus flower in Eve's hair or Adam eating mango doesn't take much imagination in this environment. The variety of tropical greenery here is undoubtedly a close second to what they had back then. Indeed, for some, it is paradise found.

But that is only part of the story. While some play, others work. As folks recline on beach chairs without worrying, some can't afford such luxury. Significant is the imbalance of wealth and privilege that is easily observable. For example, Naples has a Ferrari dealership next door to a Wal-Mart.

Under the shade of ever-present palm trees, there is a playground for "the haves," "almost haves," and "have some things, sometimes." Workers languish in the heat while tourists sip on sugary cocktails. Here is the paradox of "paradise" outside mythic Eden, simultaneously, it is found and lost.

Even for those with privileged access, paradise is elusive. The perfect harmony and peace that characterized Eden are long gone. Brokenness in mind, body, and spirit persists within the human creature and infects all our relationships. We have literally and figuratively polluted our world and lives. Adam and Eve's mistake repeats as humanity pursues self-centered schemes for power, glory, and prominence.

Authentic paradise is beyond our reach, capacity, and agency. No matter how hard we seek, we will never find it; no matter our efforts to construct it, we will remain unable to do so. And so we are left with partial alternatives that, at best, offer mere glimpses of God's intended Eden.

And that will have to do until that day when we come to the end of our life's road, and God takes us into paradise untainted and unrestricted. In hope, we cling to Christ's promise to the thief who hung on the cross when he said, "Today, you will be with me in paradise (Luke 23:43)." By the grace of God, Christ will welcome us home with divine aloha.

Meanwhile, we have some living to do. In partial paradises near and far, with and without palm trees, God invites us to live with purpose, meaning, and in the context of love. This invitation aligns with that deep longing within us that Augustine described as the restless search for God.

For over twenty-five years as a pastor serving Christian communities in three states, I continue to see this desire in those I encounter. Folks want connection and purpose-filled living. They want to make a difference and do more than survive. It is no different in Southwest Florida among those who come for a while and those who live here year-round. Like everywhere else, there is a need for belonging and love.

Although much can be purchased here that brings happiness, authentic joy can not. The biblical witness convinces me that joy must come from more profound places deep within the heart of loving relationships with God and others. You can't buy that in a store or online.

When found, joy and love create a paradise of their own. For a moment, Eden is restored as our Creator's original intention and desire for balance, harmony, and peace becomes realized. I pray this book will offer glimpses of paradise as you seek and find God.

CHAPTER ONE:
WAVES

"A great windstorm arose, and the waves beat into the boat, so that the boat was already being swamped. But he was in the stern, asleep on the cushion; and they woke him up and said to him, "Teacher, do you not care that we are perishing?" He woke up and rebuked the wind, and said to the sea, "Peace! Be still!" Then the wind ceased, and there was a dead calm."

Mark 4:37-39

Waves are curious, powerful, and inspiring. They are always in motion—coming and going—and vary in intensity. We can run into them, ride upon them, and dive under them. Waves can simultaneously lift us up or pull us down, carrying us onward or stopping our journey.

In addition to physical interaction, waves can connect with our emotions and souls. Something is calming about the cadence of crashing surf. Listening to waves, we can drift off to sleep or chill out.

I have spent hours watching the waves as they come ashore. Looking and listening while I sit in my beach chair is relaxing. Most days, the scene is peaceful, inviting reflection and rest. Aided by a few deep breaths, cares and worries seem to melt away.

I have also found that waves renew my spirit. My spiritual imagination is excited by the circular energy exerted upon water, moving up and down, back and forth. Repeatedly and rhythmically, our lives rise and fall in the context of a relationship with the Creator of the Universe.

Daily, there is the potential to connect with our Creator upon the tides of routines, storms, and calm. When we do, we experience the joy of renewal as unexplainable peace washes over us. We can drift without care upon the waters that glisten with hope.

How do we play and splash in these beautiful and generative waters? How do we wash away the dirt that clings to our spirits and demeans us with lies about our worthiness? How do we cleanse ourselves from insecurities and the micro-aggressions we and others smear on us?

Waves of God's love can carry away the negative soil that accumulates upon us, making us feel less of the person God created us to be. Refreshed in grace, we can start with a new perspective and understanding of our identity as a child of God.

Loved and lovely, we are free of the debris that floats our way.

Daily, there is also the danger of rip tides, choppy waters, and fears of sharks that lurk below the surface. Waves aren't easily controlled - at least not by us. The chaos of storms, near and far, pull and tug at the tides, increasing the ferocity and intensity of the water that crashes upon the shore. We must pay attention and exercise caution in the face of powerful forces.

When life's tide brings danger, we need protection and wisdom. Once again, our faith is a resource. Seeking God as chaos rises and falls around us, we yearn for a safe haven. Trusting in God's promise of presence, prayer can remind us that we are not alone. God remains with us, and God's power is beyond our understanding. Scripture can provide an encouraging word for our drenched and discouraged spirits. Over the centuries, God's people have found courage in these sacred words. As proverbial waves crest over the bow, we have resources to weather the storms and navigate threatening waters.

More than once, the waves have inspired me to wonder about my baptismal connection with God. The constant motion of the tide matches the flow of grace into and out of my life, washing back and forth. Love comes with the power of forgiveness and the beckoning call of response. Here is the paradox of being renewed and disturbed. Waves of love bless and bother.

Following Jesus is not an exercise in personal fulfillment, betterment, and self-affirmation. Of course, these things happen, but that is not the goal of discipleship. God loves us with a purpose - that love might flow through us. We are a channel or inlet through which God's grace, love, forgiveness, and mercy pass. Our words and actions become the vehicle through which God's reign swells into a world that resists such measures.

At once, I am refreshed and reminded that I'm not alone. In addition to the dynamic connection with God, I can't escape the reality that my wave is not the only one in the ocean. The crest of my wave is but one of many. My movement links me with that of others. We sometimes journey in parallel fashion, heading to the shore perfectly. At other times, there is clash and conflict. We bounce into each other. Crash! Splash!

More angry and choppy waters are bound to crash over us as we extend compassion and kindness, seek biblical justice for those who are outcasts and prejudged, work for peace and reconciliation, and care for a vulnerable creation. Why? Forces of self-interest, tribal loyalty, privilege, and arrogance resist God's ways with fear, hatred, seduction, and violence. As the power brokers, religious zealots, and hardliners responded to Christ's teaching and preaching with crucifixion, so are Christ's followers met with suffering and struggle.

Following Christ can be bothersome, the moment love begins to flow beyond ourselves. Comfort zones fade fast as we see the world through different eyes. We can no longer disregard or ignore the faces of others we may not recognize, dislike, or disagree with. Love your neighbor. Love your enemy. These Jesus-teachings prod us in ways that we might not naturally respond to.

Love begs us to lower our guard, share what we have, and become vulnerable. Like the child who rushes into the wave at the beach, we may lose our footing, wipe out, and get sand in our shorts.

In this chapter, waves will guide our reflection about what it means to be a baptized child of God. We will seek God's presence as proverbial waves rise and fall about us. We will seek wisdom from beyond the horizon. Following Christ to the best of our ability, we will seek joy from being in a relationship with God and expanding relationships with others.

Even paradise has days when the weather is less than perfect. On one such "chilly" afternoon, I went to the beach. Grey clouds permeated the ashen sky.

Looking to the horizon, I saw the waves topped with whitecaps.

My mind wandered. I wondered what it must have been like to have been the disciple Andrew on that day when the storm arose on the Sea of Galilee, and Jesus was asleep in the boat. What were Andrew's thoughts as he watched the approaching wind and waves? Maybe they went something like this...

I don't like the look of that approaching cloud. The rapidly advancing storm shelf is dark and foreboding. That was never good. I have been a fisherman upon these waves for most of my life. What a strange "lake" this is - more like a sea. It is such a vast body of water it always seems to have a mind of its own. One moment, it can be calm and peaceful, with waves no more than gentle ripples. Sometimes, the sea can be angry with massive waves that curl and batter.

Although you can never be sure how the waves will be, I have always tried to read the signs and portents of lousy weather. When the sky darkens, as it is doing quickly, trouble is coming. Now is the time to secure loose items and tie down the sail. Since we are too far from the shore, we must ride out the storm.

I can feel the rain start—one drop, then another. Soon, the heavens will open, and the deluge will begin. My experience tells me that it will be a long and challenging night.

As the water falls upon my head, I prepare for the storm, grab the boat's gunwale, and prepare for the worst. Here it comes! We are beginning to bounce violently up and down. The crest of the waves looms higher than our heads, providing a canopy of doom. Bilge quickly swells and fills the bottom of the boat.

The wind and waves have an intensity that I've not seen before. It is as though I am in the primordial chaos itself. These are not ordinary elements but the vile tools of evil forces that threaten to drown out life itself. The waves crash over the boat with the fury of demons and monsters determined to destroy the craft and all inside.

It reminds me of the most recent of the clashes between Jesus and Satan's minions. We attended worship on the sabbath when this man started shrieking and convulsing. The poor man was out of his mind - possessed. It was a frightening sight. Shouting vile words that made no sense, he hissed, spat, and snarled inhumanly.

His jerking movements toward our Master were threatening. We clenched our fists, ready for a fight. With twelve of us, I was sure we'd subdue him. Our teacher would be safe even if it meant a few cuts and bruises. I could read my brother Peter's mind - bring it on!

Instead of turning away from the oncoming assault, Jesus advanced toward the tormented soul. Looking into the sorrowful eyes of that pitiful creature, Jesus calmed the storm raging within his very being. His strong words demanded the demons to leave. As they did, a calmness appeared. We watched the miracle of restoration before our eyes. Life and normalcy returned. Joy replaced tension and fear in that holy place. Through Jesus, God created anew.

BOOM! CRACK! Thunder and lightning bring me back to the present. The sea drenches my robe. Waves pour over my body and fill the bottom of the boat. My brother Peter is now on his knees, bucketing water. It is futile work, considering the volume and intensity of the angry waves. With the water level over our ankles, we will soon be underwater. Although all hands have joined in the struggle to hold on and bail out - we are losing the battle. It would take a miracle to survive.

Which brings me to wonder, where is Jesus? Where is the one who fought the demons and restored life to miserable victims of chaos and disorder? Where is the strong voice that commands and creates life?

While these questions swirl, joy evades, and fear surges within. I am flailing as death is drowning out life.

Peter, Matthew, Judas - have you seen Jesus? Where is he? Doesn't he care that we are all about to die?

With a dread to match the storm's severity, I look and find the answer to my frantic question - Jesus lies sleeping in the boat's stern.

The story will continue...

The loud surf interrupts my imaginative thoughts of Andrew. Boom, crash! The sound reminds me I am standing on the shore facing agitated waves. Nature isn't always serene and soothing. There are times when we face irritation and opposition.

In my first Lenten season as a pastor serving a congregation in Southwest Florida, I decided it would be a neat experience to invite others to join me on the beach at sunset. After the sun melted into the Gulf waves, we could close the day with a simple prayer of gratitude.

Why not make the most of the beauty of one's surroundings? For many who are vacationing and snowbirding, sunsets on the beach are on the "must-do" list. For those who live year-round in the area and who may not have gone to the beach in a while, it would be a reminder of maybe why they moved here in the first place. Either way, it was a no-cost, easy way of bringing folks together to do something most people enjoy.

Having spent many satisfied Sunday nights where the waves meet the shore, I anticipated a successful outcome. Of all the complicated and detailed events I've planned, this was not. Bring your chair. Meet at the beach. Watch the waves. Relax. Smile. Joy. What could go wrong?

Red Tide. Red Tide is the common name for harmful algal blooms. These are colonies of algae growing out of control that can produce toxic effects on people, marine life, and birds. As the name suggests, this algae can turn the water red. Although these blooms have been found in the Gulf for years, increasing frequency worries scientists, those who live along the coast, and those who depend upon tourist dollars. If you want to see what it looks like and learn more, check out the National Oceanic and Atmospheric Administration (NOAA) website[2].

When I first heard about Red Tide, I was suspicious. The news reports sounded to me like a bloom of alarmist media. Pictures of dead fish floating and cloudy conditions seemed sensational.

I decided to proceed with the Lenten gathering at the beach. Attendance was, after all, optional. If folks were concerned about the color of the tide, they would choose to stay home, and I would meet those who weren't concerned.

After parking the car, I walked toward the beach with a chair and cooler. About a block away, I

---

[2] https://oceanservice.noaa.gov/hazards/hab/gulf-mexico.html

could feel a roughness in my throat. Cough. Cough. I kept walking. The coughing continued.

Arriving at the beach, I noticed a haze hovering over the sand and waves. Cough. Cough. I set up the chair and looked at the waves. There wasn't any red coloring that I could see, but something was in the air, and it was not friendly.

A few others, who were also occasionally coughing, joined my wife and me to watch the sunset. It was as pretty as usual, except the overall experience was lacking. Whereas I usually like to sit for a while after sunset, we packed up as soon as the sun faded into the horizon.

Walking back to the car, I continued coughing until I reached about a block from the beach. Then, as suddenly as it began, the coughing stopped. I could breathe again—no doubt, Red Tide is real. Even though I could not see the "red," the waves offshore carried the bloom. The toxins the bloom produces on the waves irritate respiratory systems - a hazardous reality for those with asthma.

Reflecting on that experience, I see how our environment can harm our health and well-being. We often find ourselves in conditions that are beyond our control. The waves roll, tides rise and fall, and algae bloom without asking my opinion, permission, or even recognition. At times, the best I can do is be aware of what is happening and respond as best I can.

Where was God in this experience? Unlike the situation with Andrew and the other disciples, Jesus didn't rebuke the Red Tide and make it disappear. One could even say that Jesus remained sleeping in the boat. Additionally, one could declare that this was an ecological matter and did not involve God.

Alternatively, the experience of Red Tide raised awareness. I looked into the issue, which has scientists and business owners concerned. What effect does pollution have on our environment and the tourist economy? Various institutions and entities are researching to find answers, a precursor to solutions. Again, some might say this does not involve God.

But it does. All matters concerning the environment have a spiritual component. After all, what happens to the creation concerns the Creator. A broken creation yearns for restoration. According to Paul's letter to the Romans, "We know that the whole creation has been groaning in labor pains until now (Romans 8:22)." Creation, like humans, needs the redemption of God, and it cries out.

Let's get back to the scientists and the business folks wrestling with the negative impact that Red Tide causes. Martin Luther once taught about the importance of vocation. Christ calls each of us to live out our faith in a loving God in the context of our workplace. Whether we acknowledge it or not,

God works through people. Our hands, hearts, and minds are available tools God can use to bring about change.

Another preacher, Frederick Buechner, describes vocation as connecting our great joy with the world's great need[3]. Applying our skills, knowledge, hard work, and imagination to meeting needs relieves a groaning creation and lends meaning and purpose to our lives. We are not all scientists, businesspeople, or even employed, but we each have something to contribute. And when we do, it is spiritual because God gave us those talents, abilities, and capacities.

Christians can link vocation with baptism. Applying our God-given gifts, we follow Jesus in ministry that impacts others and creation. Although some ministry happens inside the church, most lies beyond steepled buildings. Our service in the world is part of God's greater creative and redeeming efforts.

In the case of the sunset watching during Red Tide, I leaned into my vocation as a pastoral leader and, based on wanting to keep folks healthy, postponed the beach ministry until the harmful algal bloom passed. When it was gone, I resumed the gathering. We managed to catch another glorious setting before Lent's end.

---

[3] Frederick Buechner, <u>Wishful Thinking; A Theological ABC</u> (Harper Collins, 1993)

Regarding the ongoing issue of Red Tide, I pray for collaborative solutions to emerge as God moves hearts, heads, and hands. Amazing things are possible when there is will and vocational application.

The constant crashing of the waves against the shoreline brings my awareness back to my walk surfside. From ecological worries and concerns much bigger than I can grasp, my attention turns to something within my control.

Mindfulness teaches intention and encourages our paying attention to breathing. Most of the time, we go about life without thinking about the most basic functions essential to survival. Human creatures need to breathe.

Thankfully, breathing happens automatically (unless environmental or health issues hamper it). It is a blessing not to think about where or if the next wave of oxygen will enter our lungs.

But life is more than mechanics. Living is more than bodily functioning. Meaning, purpose, and joy come from a place beyond our ability to inhale and exhale air. These are matters of not body alone but body and spirit.

When we focus and center ourselves, paying attention to our breathing, something opens within us. We become aware of not only our body's functioning but also the connection between ourselves, our environment, those around us, and our Creator.

It is important to recall that in the Bible, the Hebrew (ruah) and Greek (pneuma) words for breath/air are the same words for spirit. The second creation story in the book of Genesis tells us that God breathed life into the human creation formed from the dirt. It was the ruah/pneuma/spirit that animated our archetypal ancestor. Likewise, it is this same spirit that continues to bring life to us.

When we stop and take a deep, cleansing, and purposeful breath, we reconnect with God's spirit, which is always present and brings us life. Stop. Inhale deeply. Hold your breath. Cherish it. Slowly exhale. Repeat. Enter into the pattern of breathing in and out. Allow the practice of breathing to be an offering of prayer—an active and wordless communication with God's Spirit.

Deep breathing while watching and hearing waves crash upon the shore is spiritually satisfying. If the beach is far away, you can close your eyes and listen to a recording of ocean waves. Coordinating your breathing with the rolling and breaking brings contentment and joy. There is a rhythm of love that washes over, cleanses, and renews.

Recalling our baptism is one way to reconnect with the constant wave of God's movement in our lives. Through those foundational spiritual waters, God promises always to be near. Love, grace, faith, forgiveness - these essential gifts of a loving God are never far away. They are as close as the breath/air/spirit that fills us multiple times a minute, whether we pay attention or not. The flow of breathing deeply and cherishing our baptismal identity renews us. Joy comes through this connection.

Sunlight on water
glistens upon each ripple
imagining sky.

Sky and water dance
where the horizon extends
timeless, eternal.

Through water and Word,
our lives rise and fall with God.
Forever linked - joy.

I am back on the beach, and the agitated waves provide the soundtrack for my evening walk. I enjoy the natural drama and rising crescendo of wave after wave crashing on the shoreline. Even though there is no storm, the surf's energy reminds me that nature isn't always tame. It can be wild and dangerous.

My mind wanders back to Andrew and the other disciples caught in the massive waves of the Sea of Galilee. I wonder if this might have occurred as Andrew, drenched with the storm, began to despair.

As the wind and waves fiercely torment our boat, I know it won't be long before we lose the battle. Above the howling and sloshing, I shout to my brother Peter—wake him up! Wake the master up!

Peter crawls through the bilge water toward the bow. I watch as he wakes our teacher. How could anyone sleep through this?

Waking, Jesus steadies himself with a hand on each side of the boat. Slowly rising on both feet, he faces the unrelenting gale.

With the same passion of that day in the synagogue, Jesus rebukes the winds and waves, "Peace, be still!"

And as the demons left the body of their victim, so did the storm's chaos depart. The winds and the waves obeyed the master by settling down immediately without a moment's hesitation. It was another miracle that rescued life!

Joy fills every part of me as I kneel on the rapidly drying deck. There are no words to describe what I have just witnessed. Only the Creator has such power to direct the movements of the sea.

The question about whether Jesus cared if we perished seems misplaced and silly. Not only does he care, he has the unimaginable power to restore. And Jesus chooses to use it.

How does one respond to such things? How will others not in this boat react when they hear what happened today? Centuries from now, when folks read these words from their sacred book, what will they think?

I'm sure some will dismiss it as another fantastic tale told by fishermen. Others will try to explain it away, concocting a rational explanation for what transpired. Still, others will receive it as an affirmation of faith.

For those who are open and seek God amid the storms of life, both literal and metaphoric, I pray that this story will bring you hope. When the wind and wave push to overcome, know Christ remains in your boat. You are never alone. Rest in the trust that the One who created you loves you and will restore you to life. Though it might seem unlikely, joy is on the other side of the fear, concern, and chaos within. Trust me, you will find joy beyond Christ's words, "Peace! Be Still!"

I sit still on my beach chair, breathing deeply, cherishing the moment, and watching the waves roll in. Joy fills me. What a beautiful day it is to be alive!

Fears and concerns seem to melt away as the sun shines above.

This scene of refreshment unlocks my memory. I am brought back to a time decades ago when my children were younger. In those days, we lived in Northcentral New Jersey, about an hour and a half away from the nearest beach.

Now and then, we would pack up the car with our gear and head to the Atlantic coast. A day at the beach was always a good time for our family. Walking in the surf, bobbing in the water, making sand castles, sitting on the sand - we did and enjoyed it all.

On one of those excursions, I remember walking with my oldest son, Noah. He was a toddler. Decked out in a bucket hat, tiny swim shorts, sandals, and a colorful T-shirt, he had the "beach thing" down. He had just mastered running, and with his little feet hurrying, he was a cute sight to see.

Together, we went for a walk at the surf's edge. Wearing sandals, we didn't want to get wet, we walked irregularly, avoiding the ocean's incoming foam. Scurrying back and forth against the advancing and receding tide, we must have looked like a pair of sandpipers.

The Atlantic Ocean can get rough, sending large waves to crash upon the sand. So it was on that day, I recall. I was nervous about my fearless son's hurried wandering in the surf zone. "Hold my hand," I insisted. And he did. His little fingers grasped my larger version. His incessant, joyful energy pulled me along.

Holding hands wasn't easy, and soon, my son's hand slipped away as he rushed through the foam toward the breaking waves. This breakaway action raised my anxiety. He was probably fine, but my parental instincts were in overdrive. "Hold my hand," I demanded as I ran to catch up with him. And he did for a little longer until the next burst of energy caused him to dart away. Our pattern repeated.

Back and forth we went. Anxieties raised and lowered. Youthful exuberance bounced up against overprotective adult concern. Play versus protection. Fear opposing joy.

I wanted Noah to be safe; twenty years later, that hasn't changed. If I could wrap him up with bubble wrap and ensure that no harm would ever come to him, I would. But I can't. It wasn't possible on that day on the beach, and it isn't today, as my "baby" has grown. You never stop worrying about your children.

But there is more; the worry and anxiety of being a parent are just part of the picture and not the most significant part. The connection, the relationship, exceeds all concerns. Whether hands are held or not, the love between parent and child binds us together. Not even a colossal tsunami could break that apart.

So, it is with us and our heavenly parent. We undoubtedly cause grief and worry in our Creator as we dart and dash in erratic directions. Our hands slip apart as we scoot away. We might even stumble in the damp sand or find ourselves wet. Amidst our breakaway behavior, we never leave God's watchful eye. We remain connected to God by the bond of love.

It took me years to realize the importance of loosening the parental grip and letting go of my need for control. I'm still learning, but I like to think that I've made strides since that day on the beach so long ago. Freedom and letting go are necessary for relationships to grow and thrive. Hovering, smothering, judging, and calling all the proverbial shots is unhealthy, limiting, and ultimately damaging to relationships.

Freedom is an important aspect of our relationship with God. God doesn't micromanage our every choice nor hover and pull the strings of blessings and curses to affect our movement. God is not a Divine Puppet Master.

Instead, we are given a will and the opportunity to behave as we choose. If we want to rush into overpowering waves, get knocked down, and be pulled out to sea by the currents, then we are free to be as foolish as we desire. Our Loving God will not stop us from making mistakes of various sizes and consequences.

Even as we live in ways that break our heavenly parent's heart, God's love remains. Our relationship with our Creator endures our foolishness and continues through the consequences of our indiscretions and failures. Ultimately, God's loving response is mercy, not judgment.

God's hand remains extended, waiting for ours to return. When that reunion happens, we regain a sense of paradise, and joy abounds.

———————

Sitting on the beach, watching the waves caress the shore, I breathe deeply. The Gulf of Mexico stretches out as far as I can see. From a hidden place beyond the horizon, the waves come to me. Each brings joy with a soothing sound that quiets my soul. Ahhhh. Calm and peace wash over me.

These waves are gentle today, but I have seen them when they weren't. Walking along these same waters days before Hurricane Ian landed was a different scene.

Although I didn't know how destructive that storm would be, you could see the intensity building in the surf.

Not only was I unaware of the coming catastrophe, but I had yet to learn of the massive power of waves and how their surge could destroy life and property. Walls of water overwhelmed communities, forever changing the landscape and lives. Some areas of Fort Myers Beach are still devastated a year and a half later.

Waves demand our respect and attention. The moment we take them for granted is when we can find ourselves washed away in them or miss their calming presence. Attention and intention remain essential responses.

Likewise, our spiritual lives require awareness. In the waters of baptism, God's love and grace wash over Christians. Baptism gives a new identity, establishing a lasting relationship with Christ. Returning and focusing on this connection strengthens and renews our faith. We find the courage to face the rise and fall, ebb and flow, back and forth of life. There is also joy found as we sense God's unrelenting presence.

Regardless of how intense they might be, the waves keep coming from the horizon to shore. Though the crest varies, all waves have a common destination— they move ashore. So, it is with God's love and care that it comes to us.

In our search to find God, it would do us well to stop, breathe, and watch. With varying intensities, in various circumstances, stormy and calm, the direction of love is toward us. God moves in our direction. Waiting in faith, trusting in the relationship God created with us upon the waters of baptism, love washes over us. Again and again. Pushing and pulling at us. Drawing us in the direction of who God created us to be.

CHAPTER TWO: SAND

"As Jesus passed along the Sea of Galilee, he saw Simon and his brother Andrew casting a net into the sea — for they were fishermen. And Jesus said to them, "Follow me and I will make you fish for people." And immediately they left their nets and followed him. As he went a little farther, he saw James son of Zebedee and his brother John, who were in their boat mending the nets. Immediately he called them; and they left their father Zebedee in the boat with the hired men, and followed him."

Mark 1:16-20

It was late in the day when I finally got to the beach. Although I had planned to arrive earlier, a combination of chores and distractions rearranged the day's itinerary. No matter, I resolved, "a late arrival at the beach is still an arrival at the beach."

Stepping off the wooden boardwalk from the parking area, my feet sank into the white sand, and I took a deep, renewing breath. Ah, beach.

Carrying my chair, I plodded onward. There is nothing graceful about schlepping beach equipment across the uneven and soft surface of the sand. Struggling to maintain balance, I scanned the beach for a place to claim.

Only a few folks were on the beach, although there was undoubtedly a larger crowd earlier in the day. You could see where children dug holes in the sand and built their sandcastles. One child even left a small plastic shovel behind at the "construction site."

Plod. Plod. Look. The pattern continued until I finally found a spot that offered a good view of the surf. Close but not too close to the edge of the returning tide.

The setup was straightforward. All I had to do was open the beach chair and put down the cooler nearby. Since the sun was no longer high and hot in the sky, there was no need for an umbrella.

As I sat on my chair, it sank into the sand.

What a curious thing sand is. Microscopic particles of limestone, coral, and shell fragments make up this non-renewable natural resource that took millions of years to create. Erosion and the constant motion of waves move it around, taking and depositing it along the way.

As a child, I delighted in molding and shaping sandcastles. When wet, sand is a fantastic temporary building material. You can make all sorts of objects, limited only by your imagination and shovel size.

These days, I am content to sit on my beach chair and stretch out my legs upon the warm, granular surface. I also like to take long walks on the hardened sand at the water's edge.

The experience of walking barefoot on wet sand calms my restless spirit and brings me joy. It is satisfying to leave footprints. Although temporary, lasting until the tide wipes them clean, the footprints mark the path taken on the beach. Footprints are evidence that I existed for a brief moment in time, leaving a trace.

On that late afternoon, as I walked the beach close to the water, I saw the traces of many feet. There were imprints of toes and heels of all sizes. Some adult-sized footprints lined up with others, leading me to speculate that there were couples who walked together. Other smaller footprints darted toward the advancing tide. Were these made by laughing children splashing in the surf? Still, other footprints were all by themselves, suggesting a solitary stroll.

Each pattern in the sand bore witness to the presence, choices, and experiences of those who walked that way before me. My feet added marks to that fleeting record of our mutual existence, and our footprints overlapped and altered previous marks.

In this chapter, using sand as a guiding metaphor, we will consider following in Jesus's footsteps. What does it mean to allow the teaching and preaching of Christ to guide us? How might the life, death, and resurrection of Jesus serve as a resource in our search for God?

Following Jesus will bring us both comfort and challenge. There will be moments of peace as our spirits rest with assurance in God's love and grace. And there will be disturbing times when we feel like we just got some sand in our shorts.

———————

As much as I love the beach, I don't like getting sand on my feet. It's not that I mind the wet stuff that washes off in the surf. But when the granules get in between my toes and stick to my heel, they stay there long after I leave the beach. Sand can easily irritate and lessen my joy. I'm also not a happy camper when the sand gets in my shoes and sandals (okay, I'm a bit fussy). Sand has clinging and abrasive qualities that I would just as soon not have to deal with.

So, I live with the tension and within the paradox of sand. I both love and hate the stuff. Sometimes simultaneously. Oooh, that warm sand feels nice as it covers my feet. Ugh, it is sticking to me, and I won't get it all off with the footwasher at the bathhouse. It will leave a messy trail from the car into the house.

No matter how much I would like the sand to behave on my neurotic terms, it does not pay attention. Sand does not cater to my desires; it operates independently of my whims. I either accept the sand's qualities or avoid the beach.

We can draw connections between the properties of sand and following Jesus. Discipleship involves conforming our lives to Jesus and accepting Christ's qualities and values, not the other way around. Love, grace, forgiveness, generosity, and mercy will stick to us and mark us. Sometimes, we might even find these values abrasive for they question our behaviors, thoughts, cultural and personal values.

Walking with the wet sand sticking to my feet, I wonder what must it have been like to be in the crowd hearing Jesus preach about God's reign and following God's uncommon path of love.

Even though Jesus's words were inspiring and brought comfort and healing to many, not everybody agreed with what he had to say. What was it like, for example, for someone rich to hear

Jesus speak of the woes that accompany wealth? Maybe it went something like this...

My name is Asher, which means happy, fortunate, and blessed. I honor God and my family through righteous living, which includes faithful attendance at the synagogue, careful observance of the Laws of Moses, and upstanding presence in the community.

It is bothersome not to be able to see this traveling preacher clearly for all the groveling crowd. Why did Jesus choose to teach while standing on our level?

My thoughts are interrupted by a woman who just bumped into me. She is yelling, "Help me, Jesus! My child is sick." Her cry is interrupted by a hacking cough, indicating that perhaps the illness has spread.

Such grit and grime; her sandy feet are kicking up dust. This lot could use a good Mikveh, a long soak in the ritual waters of purification. That's what they need. Go wash up and then come back if you really must.

If they can't listen to Moses, what makes them think they will follow what Jesus teaches?

Precisely, what was Jesus teaching?

I guess that's why I'm here in this crowd: to hear for myself. My skepticism needs satisfying, so I'll get a little closer. I will need to push and shove my way through these heathens.

These people need to make way for their betters. According to my moral compass, I deserve the opportunity to listen more than they do.

Finally, I can see him. He looks so plain, so unassuming. Now, only if I could hear what he is saying...

I can't believe I heard Jesus say, "But woe to you who are rich, for you have received your consolation." Did Jesus just condemn wealth?

How dare he! Riches were, after all, the accepted gauge for determining divine favor. Those who followed in the ways of God's laws were the recipients of God's blessing.

I listened to all I needed to hear; it was past time to leave. The sooner I can extradite myself, the better. But I can't. In the few minutes that I listened to Jesus, the crowd closed in all around. I am shoulder to shoulder with "them."

I am ready to crawl into my skin. As soon as I escape, I will join efforts with my Pharisee friends. They were right. This Jesus is trouble.

We must stop Jesus.

What would happen if all of these miscreants became his disciples? There would be riots and revolts. The Roman Empire would not tolerate it.

The story will continue...

The following fictional story is a composite of stories heard following Hurricane Ian.

Evelyn stayed as long as she could before she evacuated her beloved dream home. Today, she does not doubt that leaving was the smart thing. After all, what defense could she have offered against the eyewall of a category-four hurricane?

Her home offered as much resistance as a sandcastle does against an advancing wave. Sadly, though of little comfort, she wasn't alone in her loss.

Hurricane Ian was catastrophic, with sustained winds of 150 mph and a 10-15 ft storm surge. Ian caused 161 fatalities and was the third costliest in US history, with losses estimated to be around $113 billion[4].

----

[4] See Hurricane Ian - Wikipedia - retrieved on 1/13/2024.

Days before Ian made landfall, Evelyn watched the weather on TV. Those weathermen are always wrong, she thought. It wouldn't be as bad as they were hyping it. Ratings are the only thing those news stations care about - Evelyn harumphed.

In the twelve years of living in southwest Florida, they got some wind and a little rain as each "storm of the century" came and went. Hurricane Irma was bad for some, but it came nowhere near her home; that was somebody else's backyard.

Walking through the damaged living room, Evelyn was numb. Disbelief combined with desperation. The surge of water turned everything upside down and inside out, and sand was all over her once immaculate home.

It wasn't supposed to happen here. The models predicted that Tampa, two hours north, would suffer the brunt of the storm. Despite her negative views on the media, Evelyn practically glued herself to the television. She couldn't get enough of the ominous coverage. Those poor folks were going to get hammered.

When the storm shifted its course, it took a while for Evelyn to realize that she was now in the target zone of 'those poor folks.' She was potentially in great danger.

Evelyn scurried to prepare as best she could. She had a neighbor put up the corrugated storm shutters over the windows - those things were too heavy and bulky. Next, the furniture came off her lanai into the living room. Evelyn checked the batteries in all her flashlights and lanterns. The power was likely to be out for a few days.

When the sky darkened, the rains began, and the wind started to rush, Evelyn was ready to hunker down and ride the storm. As the storm's intensity rose, she no longer doubted the meteorologists. Instead of disparaging their knowledge, she clung to their every word. When the word came to evacuate, Evelyn didn't hesitate.

She ran to her bedroom and grabbed some clothes; a couple of days was all Evelyn could fit into her suitcase. Locking the front door, she got into her car and drove north.

As the wipers swished back and forth, she called a friend who lived in Georgia. Roselyn always said, "if you ever need a place to escape those coastal storms, my door is open." Never in her wildest imagination did Evelyn think she would take Rosy up on her offer.

On the drive up north, Evelyn prayed out loud. The car's wipers couldn't keep up with the sheet of rain that limited visibility. She had to slow down the vehicle a few times to maintain control. Each time, her praying increased. A lifelong follower of Jesus,

Evelyn knew the power of prayer and its ability to calm her troubled soul.

A week later, Evelyn was grateful for a friend's kindness and hospitality. Rosy provided refuge from the storm and a shoulder to cry on as the first damage reports returned. Evelyn spoke with a neighbor who didn't evacuate.

The downed tree on her roof was the least of her problems. The storm surge had invaded the entire first level of the block, covering everything in sight with ten feet of water. As the water rose, her neighbor retreated to a second-story level. Thank God she survived.

There was a sandy silt that covered and ruined all of Evelyn's possessions. How would she ever recover from this? Surrounding her were a lifetime of memories, pictures, and keepsakes - all gone, destroyed.

She kept repeating, as though she needed to remind herself, "It's only things. I'm alive, and these are only things."

Evelyn's friends found her standing in the middle of her living room. They took one look at her and the grimy, disheveled room and joined her heartache. With shovels, work gloves, and water bottles, the friends came to help. But first, they hugged in silence as words failed.

———————

Scooping up a handful of sand, I notice that the grains of sand vary in color, shape, and coarseness.

On a crowded day at the beach, like you might find during Spring Break, there are people as far as you can see. Even the quickest glance around reveals a diversity of humanity. With diverse peoples comes an even greater complexity of relationships.

Friends come in all shapes, sizes, and dependability. Some friendships have stood the test of time, while others are temporary. Everyday struggles and experiences will bring folks together in the most unlikely friendships.

On the other hand, trials and tribulations can also tear friends apart, so they never speak with each other again. A difference of opinion or perceived slight can open a wound between folks that never heals.

Someone once said that the difference between family and friends is that you get to pick your friends. For the most part, that is true. When it comes to the relationship of friendship, we decide who we want to be with. We choose our real friends. They are more than "friendly" acquaintances; somehow, whether for a long or brief time, their lives link to ours. They are a second family.

The connection of friendship requires nurturing and care. Since each friendship is different, each will require differing amounts of attention. Some friendships are complex and high maintenance, while others are easy-going and flow effortlessly.

Many, including myself, love the old-time hymn "What a Friend We Have in Jesus." Imagining Jesus near and accompanying us as a good friend offers comfort. Jesus won't let us down or abandon us. No matter what we face, we will never be alone because of our friendship with Christ.

The biblical stories of Jesus and his followers inspire such thinking. Jesus ate with all sorts of folks. These meals were transformative, connecting regular people's lives with Jesus's. Joy is a critical part of these stories. Connected to Christ, friends with Jesus, there is the experience of celebratory joy.

According to New Testament scholar Hal Taussig, *Festive Joy* was a desired outcome of the Greco-Roman banquet, which provided the cultural context for early Christian gatherings. Throughout the Roman Empire, banquets were significant events that fostered friendships, provided needed social bonding, maintained social status, and strengthened the very values on which society depended. Commerce, government, status, and religion depended on the bonding in banquets[5].

When Jesus ate with folks, he was doing more than having a meal. Given the context of the Roman banquet, Jesus's table fellowship created an alternate community that depended upon a different set of values.

Jesus formed a community based on love, acceptance, inclusion, and forgiveness - values in stark contrast to Roman notions of power, might, masculinity, privilege, wealth, and hierarchy. Christ shared the values of a Loving God across boundaries of gender, class, ability, health, and wealth. Eating with tax collectors and "sinners" redefined who was welcome in the sight of God.

The joy experienced at the tables Jesus hosted was felt by those not usually accustomed to the celebratory joy of the Roman banquets to which they didn't have invitations. It was especially true for the marginalized followers of Jesus.

The invitation to the banquet and the friendship found at the table, whether Jesus's or other Roman meals, was only part of the story. Feasting together created friendships and joy, but it also created obligations and expectations.

---

[5] See In the Beginning Was the Meal (Fortress Press, 2009) by Hal Taussig. You might also be interested to read Paul Bradshaw's, Eucharistic Origins (Wipf and Stock Publishers, 2012).

Reciprocity was part and parcel of the cultural form of the banquet. Those who dined scrupulously at the table were in debt to the host. They would need to invite the host to their next banquet. If they didn't have the means to host a banquet, they would have to pay back the debt in other ways.

Similar expectations exist today. One night, you go to a friend's house for dinner. Next time, you have them over to your house. Even though you may not keep score, the relationship will likely strain if the hosting is one-sided. Extenuating circumstances such as illness, significant life changes, etc., might allow for temporary imbalance, but eventually, equilibrium returns or things might fall apart.

When Jesus shared table fellowship with tax collectors and "sinners," he extended God's friendship and love with them and formed a social obligation. The expectation was they would go and do likewise. Share love and grace with others. Feed the hungry, poor, and those who can't pay you back so you don't generate further reciprocity. A pay-it-forward understanding gave those early Christian communities a reputation for hospitality, compassion, and engagement with the poor, widows, and orphans[6].

So it is with following Jesus. God's love comes to us in Christ as a pure and unconditional gift. There is nothing we can do to earn it or manufacture it.

[6] See Christine D Pohl's book, Making Room; Recovering Hospitality as a Christian Tradition (Wm. B. Eerdmans Publishing, 1999).

Feasting on such goodness is a joyful experience. Full of joy, we want to reciprocate. We can't help ourselves.

Or at least that is the theory. God feeds us, and then we feed others; love reciprocates love, kindness produces kindness, and generosity beckons generosity. This process expands community and connection with Christ.

We break the cycle by claiming God's love as a private treasure. When our pride and arrogance receive God's grace as our deserved reward, we hijack Jesus's intentions to spread God's reign to the ends of the earth. We stop following Jesus's teachings, example, and table fellowship practices, and our joy lessens.

Sadly, we are not the only ones guilty of not following Jesus. Throughout history, the church has followed paths other than God's loving way. We've judged, excluded, condemned, and even burned a few at the stake. Not all the time, but some of the time. Not all followers of Jesus, but some who professed to be.

Whether we are talking about our response or the church's, there is a need for a continued spirit of repentance. We need to turn again and again to God, seeking God's ways and God's teachings. We need to look anew at the table fellowship of Jesus to see what faithful hosting looks like.

As we do, we will connect our friendship with Jesus with that of following Jesus - and there will be joy for us and others. It will be the kind of lasting joy we have experienced when we are in the presence of an authentic friend.

Each step upon the sand leaves a mark;
for a short while, these tiny grains tell a story.

From waters of baptism, followers of Jesus embark,
Each step upon the sand leaves a mark.

Children of light travel love's path into the dark,
guided by faith, moving outward, not seeking glory.

Each step upon the sand leaves a mark;
for a short while, these tiny grains tell a story.

When I moved to Florida, I thought I would no longer worry about trekking muck into my car. I was mistaken. There might not be wet snow and slush upon snow boots and galoshes to contend with, but sand is something as sinister.

Sand can be like the glitter children liberally sprinkle on their construction paper creations. It gets everywhere and is extremely difficult, if not impossible, to eliminate. Once sand gets in your car, it lingers in cracks and crevices, resisting even the most powerful vacuums.

Sand's persistent nature illustrates what can happen when an idea wiggles into our minds. Unexpectedly, we can find ourselves open to things we never imagined.

Let's return to the imaginative character of Asher, a wealthy and curious listener in the crowd as Jesus preached about God's place in our lives. Although initially incensed and angered when Jesus's teaching challenged him about his wealth and privilege, what might unfold if part of the message started to work on him?

Why is Jesus looking my way? Does he suspect that I am plotting against him? He seems to be smiling at me.

Strangely, there is no evil or maliciousness in his grin.
There is an unsettling authenticity. It is as though Jesus can read my ill intentions, yet he still reaches out with compassion.

Though I am the enemy of what he preaches, he appears to offer love. Jesus's whole being seems to embody his words.

Now I hear more of his words, "do good to those who hate you, bless those who curse you, pray for those who abuse you. If anyone strikes you on the cheek, offer the other also; and from anyone who takes away your coat do not withhold even your shirt."

Instead of singling me out and turning me over to the mob, Jesus's eyes hold a sympathetic gaze.

I do not need his sympathy! I am wealthy, intelligent, and connected. God has blessed me with riches. I am righteous and law-abiding. Jesus looks at me as though I am not free but as trapped as the surrounding huddled masses.

More words come from his mouth, "Give to everyone who begs from you; and if anyone takes away your goods, do not ask for them again. Do to others as you would have them do to you."

This teaching is not sedition or falsehood. It is nothing new but nestled in the heart of God. Love God with all your being and love your neighbor as yourself. That IS the law.

Accompanying his loving gaze, I detect a nodding of Jesus's head. Does he know that I've not always followed the spirit of the law? That I turned away from those in need? That I've hoarded blessings when I should have shared them?

Suddenly, I don't feel as confident in my goodness and righteousness in my relationship with God.

Maybe I need God's healing grace as much as those around me.

I look again into that loving face. This time, I see something different. It is an invitation - come and see what joy life can contain as you follow me.

What is this strange feeling lingering inside that compels me to follow?

Large piles of sand lined Bonita Beach Road in the aftermath of Hurricane Ian. Heavy construction vehicles with large bucket loaders created them by removing the deposited sand from the Gulf's receding surge water.

Although the clean-up effort began in earnest, it would take months of hard work before progress would be sufficient to allow folks to return to their homes and beach getaways.

In addition to the big bucket-loaders, giant haulers drove the roadways for months. These specially designed trucks consisted of two high-sided boxes, open on top, with a crane between them. Like fishing trawlers, they would creep slowly along the streets, scooping up the piles of debris.

Everywhere you looked, there were heaps of ruined possessions at the ends of driveways and along the roads. Refrigerators, furniture, soaked boxes, dirty linens, couches, and easy chairs were now junk. Also on the piles were broken wood, metal, trash, tiles, palm branches, and indeterminable muck. Personal items such as pictures, collectibles, and toys occasionally punctuated the rubble, accentuating the hardship and heartache.

While trash and sand piles cluttered the shoulder of the roads awaiting pickup by the heavy machines, they grew daily through the efforts of residents and volunteers. Neighbors came out to help the recovery effort, and groups of glove-clad helpers carted the destroyed remnants to the curb. There was no shortage of goodwill in the clean-up.

In addition to the grassroots efforts, relief organizations offered aid. Government assistance came from federal, state, and local sources. Churches gathered generous offerings to assist with the response. Handouts included water bottles, clothes, food, and financial support. Communities came together across divisions to cooperate.

A year later, there is still evidence of Hurricane Ian's destruction. The negative impact of the storm will linger as workers continue to repair homes, insurance claims continue through litigation, businesses struggle to reopen, building lots remain empty, and public facilities are still not fully open.

Recovery and restoration efforts can go only so far. It is like the children's storybook tale of Humpy Dumpty. All the king's horses and all the king's men couldn't put Humpy Dumpty together again. Hurricanes change communities because even the most resilient communities can't put all the pieces back together in the same way that they were before the storm's destruction.

It is sad to watch sand castles disappear into the ocean. Compassion begs empathy for those whose lives have shifted adversely. Ian's victims still need kindness, patience, understanding, and assistance. This need persists even after the relief and disaster response groups leave, the debris piles are gone, and a new season of tourists arrives with no memory of the devastation.

In the aftermath of a sizeable storm, there is always opportunity. For some, this consists of financial gain as they trade in others' sorrow. But that is not the extent of the opportunity. A greater chance exists for Jesus' followers, and that is to love.

Inspired by his teaching, followers of Jesus can use their resources for good and help in the rebuilding efforts. There is a role to play, from physically clearing debris and providing financial support to relief efforts to accompanying victims with a listening presence. Love is more than an emotion; it is an action that takes many forms.

Followers of Jesus have both the opportunity and God's invitation to provide tangible assistance to those broken and hurting. We have a greater impact when we come together as a Christian community.

Although we might feel powerless, like a speck of sand, in the face of overwhelming disaster, it would serve us well to remember that we are never alone. In Christ, God connects us to uncountable millions of other grains of sand. Together, we form a beach, a place where the water meets the land, where folk can
walk, play, and savor life.

And as we gather, we have the promise of God's presence. God shows up and empowers our service, heals our wounds, and brings us peace that exceeds our understanding. Together with God, we will find joy even in the largest piles of sand.

Sitting with legs sprawled out on the beach, I feel the sun's rays beating down from above and the warmth of the sand underneath. It is a pleasant feeling, and it invites a sigh of relief. Breathing deeply, I am relaxed. Cares and worries melt through me into the absorbent ground.

I am grateful that our local state park beach finally reopened after Hurricane Ian. Amidst all the commercial and residential development of southwest Florida, the state parks preserve patches of natural coastline for the general public's enjoyment.

Although I am not alone with my beach chair and umbrella, I settle into myself.

Surrounding me are scads of people, each with equipment to mark their spot on the sand. As far as the eye can see, there are beach chairs, blankets, coolers, umbrellas, and pop-up shelters.

Looking around, I see various ways of enjoying a beach day. Some nap under slivers of shade, while others expose their backs to get a tan. Children dig holes in the sand with bright shovels and mold castles from plastic buckets. Teenagers try out their new boogie boards in the gentle surf. Sweethearts from every generation walk holding hands. In the designated fishing area, anglers cast, Frisbees fly, and balls toss. Laughter and music form a background cacophony underlaid by the rhythmic crashing of waves.

It is another beautiful day on the beach.

I smile and take it all in, allowing the joy that encloses me on all sides to seep into my being. I lean back and close my eyes beneath the shade of my floppy bucket hat. Breathing deeply, I lean into silent and contemplative prayer.

There is so much to rejoice about. Joy follows each blessing, and there are many to name. That is not to say that my life is perfect—it is not. Nor can I claim that my life is whole with nothing broken—it is not.

Following Jesus's teachings is hard, especially when I share love, and others do not return the love. Doubts creep in and push away sacred certainties. There is much that challenges me, threatens me, and at times overwhelms me.

The sand on which my legs rest is soft and warm, offering comfort and pleasure. However, it is also abrasive and clings to my skin. The fine sand of the Gulf will stick for days and linger even after you think you have brushed it all off.

Our experience with sand is not unlike our experience following Jesus. Sometimes, we feel comforted by the assurance that God's compassion shines upon us and warms us up. Jesus' love embraces us and molds around us. What joy this brings!

At other times, however, Jesus's teachings seem rough as they scrap away at our self-interest, pride, biases, and willfulness. Our inward focus and lack of compassion for others (particularly those on the margins of our interest and experience) cause sorrow.

We need adjustment in attitude, perspective, and practice. The grit of Jesus's prophetic word has smoothing work to do on our hearts, minds, and bodies. Though it may not be fun, such activity ultimately leads to joy as it builds others up, creates/renews relationships, and forms a community centered in love.

Last, following Jesus doesn't end; it lingers. Just as it is not easy to brush off the fine grains of sand, so is the call to follow Jesus not easily swept off. The Spirit of God relentlessly pursues us in love to mold and shape our lives in the graceful image of Christ.

We are constantly becoming the children God created us to be. Although we might try to escape our true selves, a restlessness will persist. As Augustine observed, our hearts are restless until they rest in thee.

CHAPTER THREE: SHOREBIRDS

"Your steadfast love, O LORD, extends to the heavens, your faithfulness to the clouds.Your righteousness is like the mighty mountains, your judgments are like the great deep; you save humans and animals alike, O LORD. How precious is your steadfast love, O God! All people may take refuge in the shadow of your wings. They feast on the abundance of your house, and you give them drink from the river of your delights.For with you is the fountain of life;in your light we see light."

Psalm 36:5-9

Holding a cup of fresh morning coffee, I sit on my lanai and watch the sunrise over the pond behind my house. This simple ritual brings joy to the start of my day. It is a sacred place and a time to breathe deeply.

While I recharge in that space, birds fly overhead and land in the water.

It is easy to become a bird lover in Southwest Florida. Close to the Gulf, waterbirds abound year-round. From Ibises to Egrets, Eagles to Ospreys, Sandhill Cranes to Herons, Pelicans to Sand Pipers, the list goes on with many varieties. Big and small, they are elegant and exotic.

You will see birds everywhere. I find it strange that you see these tropical feathered friends when you visit regular, everyday places like a supermarket, gas station, or a home center. You don't need to go to a zoo. In fact, at the Naples Zoo, many of the exotic birds are not in a cage. They fly in for the day and enjoy the popcorn like the other visitors.

There are so many unique and unknown avian species that my wife Katie and I got ourselves a book of Southwest Florida birds. Learning bird names has opened our eyes and hearts to their diversity. What a rich and varied world God has created!

It is a truth that is more than just for birds! Humans are also diverse. We are different sizes and shapes on the outside and have assorted perspectives and passions on the inside. Our numerous experiences have made us unique beings. Like the prints on our fingers, no two patterns are alike. God made us wonderfully different.

Yet, God created us all in God's image. The *Imago Dei* is a foundational scriptural truth; "So God created humankind in his image, in the image of God he created them; male and female he created them (Genesis 1:27)." All humanity bears a piece of

God's identity. Granted, this is easier to see in the lives of some. But all have it. Even the most obnoxious, self-centered, arrogant, and hateful curmudgeon has the spark of the Creator hidden somewhere within.

The challenge we sometimes miss is to withhold judgment and show mercy. When someone grates us the wrong way, Jesus teaches us to show mercy and grace. Forgiveness comes into play when the words and actions of another bring us hurt. All these Christ-centered values can be hard to put into practice. Life is complex and messy.

Our increasingly divided culture offers little support to a life that seeks to love neighbors and enemies. A competitive, winner-takes-all mentality threatens communal well-being. Individualism, long a prized American value, runs rampant and unchecked by concern for the common good.

Social media outlets complicate matters by creating echo chambers that echo our previously held convictions, buying patterns, and political leanings. Within these chambers, we encounter "news" suited (crafted and created) for us. Lies abound and perpetuate with each posting and reposting.

It is getting harder to flock together with birds of a different feather.

Although some welcome the division and cultural segregation, our strained reality runs up against

God's dream. The prophet Isaiah, speaking God's Word, imagines a time when the nations - which is "bible speak" for 'everyone from every part of the globe - shall come together at God's feast.

"On this mountain the LORD of hosts will make for all peoples a feast of rich food, a feast of well-aged wines, of rich food filled with marrow, of well-aged wines strained clear. And he will destroy on this mountain the shroud that is cast over all peoples, the sheet that is spread over all nations; he will swallow up death forever. Then the Lord GOD will wipe away the tears from all faces, and the disgrace of his people he will take away from all the earth, for the LORD has spoken. It will be said on that day, Lo, this is our God; we have waited for him, so that he might save us. This is the LORD for whom we have waited; let us be glad and rejoice in his salvation."

Isaiah 25:6-9

God's dreams are global, inclusive, and expansive. The Bible imagines a future where tribes stop battling over territory and resources. Some lives and tears will no longer count more than others. God will equally recognize all who suffer and wipe away everyone's tears. We will all feast together with God, leaving no one out.

It will be like a giant rookery, with birds of various species coming together. God's many flocks will nest, rest, and fly together.

Most mornings, a colony of Ibis greets me with a flyover. These distinctive birds have slim, curved beaks that look like drinking straws and come in either black or white. This particular colony is primarily black; they are "Glossy Ibis." However, two White Ibis hang out with them.

Hanging out with different species is not something that "tribally-minded" humans are all that comfortable with or skilled at. At the time of Jesus, Jews and Samaritans didn't get along with each other. Okay, that is a bit understated. They disliked, distrusted, and discounted each other as often as opportunities presented. Since they were distant relatives, separated by complex historical realities, the bad relations were bitter and irreconcilable, or so their traditions taught.

Jesus's ministry and teaching challenged all forms of tribal exclusiveness. A classic example is the parable about a Good Samaritan. In a radical twist, the Samaritan is the hero of the story. The Samaritan, not the holy characters in the parable, understands the most basic ethical tenet of the faith—love thy neighbor.

Because of the deep division between Jews and Samaritans, I wonder how the one who was robbed, beaten, and left for dead might have thought about the lack of help from his own tribe.

Let's imagine together that the victim stirs under the covers in a roadside inn. The bandages wrapped around his head are caked with blood and unable to contain the throbbing of his skull. He awakens and starts to piece together his ordeal. Might it have gone something like this?

Where am I? Why am I in this bed? What are these bandages doing around my hands? Around my head?

I can't think or move. My body aches. I keep drifting in and out of consciousness.

As I do, images pop into my head. I'm walking along the road to Jericho. Large boulders line the rocky path. It is a dangerous place, known for robbers and wild animals lying in wait. Ambushes are frequent and often deadly.

My memory returns to me.

A few days ago, I was walking on the Jericho road, heading back from a very lucrative business in Jerusalem. The bag that I wore slung across my shoulder weighed down with shekels. I had one hand on the small dagger tucked inside my cloak and another on the walking staff. Anticipating trouble, I was ready for an attack along this highway through the wilderness.

How, then, did it happen? From where did the robbers come?

Thieves have an uncanny ability to sense opportunity: a weak lock, an unattended treasure, a distracting commotion. Patient, they wait for the right moment to strike and snatch. The more patient and cunning they are, the longer they remain uncaught. Like a crocodile lying on the banks of the Nile, they appear lifeless and pose no apparent threat until they lunge into action.

They must have been waiting behind the huge rocks at the curve in the road. I certainly didn't see them. In a flash, I was on the ground; I no longer held my dagger or staff. Defenseless, I fell victim to their beating blows. Curling up into a ball, I futilely attempted to protect myself. It was no use. Blood, my blood, started to stain the dirt. Pain throbbed in my head and sides as the blows continued.

At some point in my attack, a hand reached into my bag and relieved me of my coins. I would have gladly given them anything they wanted if they would have stopped. But they didn't ask, nor did they cease. I blacked out.

The memory brings terror back to my body.

It was some time before I regained awareness. I recall feeling the sun beating upon my wrecked body, which my attackers left for dead on that rocky road. Maybe they yielded their prey to the vultures and wild dogs. Unable to move, I was an easy offering. Moaning, I announced my presence to a nightmarish fate.

Adonai, help me! Have mercy upon me. Deliver me from my enemies.

My desperate, endless prayer was paused only by the lapse of consciousness. Time lost all meaning as the heat level rose and suffering increased.

During one stretch of alertness, I saw a shadowy figure in the distance. It cautiously approached along the narrow road. When my blurry vision came into focus, I saw a priest. It was an answer to prayer! Praise Adonai!

Imagine my joy when I noticed one of those who conducted the sacrifices at Yahweh's dwelling place, the Temple in Jerusalem. It was a miracle from the storehouse of God's steadfast love and faithfulness! What favor Yahweh sent upon me!

The difference between blessings and curses often lies within our interpretation. As events play out, further clarification unfolds. My initial perception of blessing proved incorrect.

After making eye contact with me, seeing my frantic plea for help, the priest averted his gaze. He pretended not to recognize my plight, cursing me by walking away briskly. I faded again as now my heart broke.

More time passed, again, I don't know how long. I blinked my heated eyelids as the sun burned an orange circle into my sight. Thirst demanded quenching. Even my blood dried up, caking on my shriveling skin.

Another person approached. Again, I was relieved he was part of my tribe, a fellow Jew. Perhaps the priest needed to maintain ritual purity for the sacrifice he would perform. Could he have sent a helper, one of the Levites that guards and takes care of the regular nonpriestly tasks required to keep the Temple in good shape and running well?

Indeed, in a hostile world, we Jews need to stick together. Yahweh's flock flew together through the storms of struggle, oppression, and near annihilation for centuries. There was surviving strength in the community that we shared.

Leaning into a common identity, I awaited a refreshing sip from the Levite's water bag as he stooped down to serve a fellow Israelite. But he didn't stop. Instead of sharing its contents, the Levite grasped the water bag closer to his chest. His other hand held a knife, and he looked nervously around. Did he think I was a decoy? Why was he afraid?

Suffering, I slipped into the darkness, abandoned by my people.

The story will continue...

The following fictional story emerged from a conversation with one of my retired colleagues who served Southwest Florida for over twenty years.

It was a big election year, and Pastor Martin served a mid-size congregation in Florida. This church was also a historic polling place on election day. Over the years, the community elected various candidates from both sides of the aisle. The results of these elections were often close, with only a few percentage points separating the victor from the loser.

Always careful not to "be political," Pastor Martin preached the gospel of God's love and grace. His church was a "purple" one with as many "red" conservatives as "blue" progressives. Naturally, this occasionally caused some tension, but Pastor Martin was skilled at keeping the focus on people and needs, not policies and partisanship. As a result, folks who vigorously opposed each other's politics could respect Pastor Martin.

His leadership kept the church together, even as the national church body became more politically progressive, taking stances that angered conservatives. The pastor would listen to their concerns about what was coming from church headquarters in Chicago and remind them that the Evangelical Lutheran Church in America was a church of three coexisting components - national, synod (regional), and local.

Each part of the ELCA church body was connected in Christ and didn't need to agree on all policy and practice matters. Church leaders in Chicago could speak their conscience to the church as a whole, but they could not dictate the conscience of a local congregation, and vice versa. Our system is not a dictatorial hierarchy but a collaborative interaction of the three expressions.

Most of the time, this answer didn't fully satisfy the anger of someone who thought that the Presiding Bishop's latest email was politically out-of-line, but it let some of the steam out of the conversation. Pastor Martin assured them they didn't need to always agree with what was said. We were a church of dialogue and discernment, not dictates and indoctrination. Lutherans could be, and were, on both sides of the political aisle, even if national leadership tipped to one side.

In recent years, however, Pastor Martin noticed it was getting harder to be in the middle. Moderate voices in both major political parties were losing ground to more extreme positions. Religious zeal was mixing with politics, fueling cultural divisions between those who wanted to return to traditions of the past and those who tried to rewrite the future and the past. In such a divisive context, ideological entrenchment labeled cooperation a sign of weakness.

Pastor Martin's phone buzzed. More Facebook posts. Friends with various people, his social media network was all over the map.

Lately, there was a lot of angry partisan chatter between a healthy dose of puppy and kitten videos. Emojis, a new word in the pastor's lexicon, flooded his screen. These word images were getting more and
more inflammatory.

Images and accusations continued throughout the hotly contested 2016 election season. False representations and fake news were everywhere. News outlets—some of which the informed pastor had never heard of—were no longer covering up their biases. The line between truth and lies blurred as echo chambers told audiences what they wanted to hear.

What made Pastor Martin especially sad were the biting remarks that his parishioners were hurling at each other. Never in a million years could he imagine these folks saying such things face to face. Online, however, they pulled no punches, holding no restraint. And they were becoming increasingly nasty to each other. The civilities on which communities depended were fading away.

It was getting harder to preach. Recently, Pastor Martin received virulent emails condemning his sermons. Like the social media posts he disparaged, the irate emails lacked respect. He couldn't believe what people thought it was okay to say to their pastor. They blamed him for pursuing a liberal agenda and not preaching the Bible. Sometimes, they would even quote scriptural interpretations from their media pundits, bible hacks who never stepped foot inside a theological institution of study. All the pastor's years of study seemed to no longer count on the front lines of this ideological battle that raged around him.

No matter how much he just wanted to preach and teach the gospel with the freedom afforded to him by his Lutheran tradition, he found himself in the middle of a cultural war that was full of landmines. The mere mention of specific phrases would ignite angry pushback and character assassination.

All this tension mounted throughout the heated presidential campaign season. Pastor Martin could see his people's anxiety rise. Folks were getting louder and bolder with their politics. Some people even began to leave the church, citing the lack of "biblical" preaching, which was code for a particular type of populist fundamentalism. These "friends" previously hosted Pastor Martin and his wife for dinner. Now, they stopped talking to the pastor. It was painful.

On the day of the election, the neighborhood, which Pastor Martin served faithfully for over a decade, came out to vote. Not wanting to mix politics and religion, obeying the election rules, he was careful not to enter the polling place. There was even a line outside the door before the doors opened.

Throughout the day, he watched the people come and go. Pastor Martin knew many of them by name. Even if he only saw them through the office window, he was glad to have been a part of their lives.

When the polls closed, Pastor Martin, who was always a good host, checked in with the polling workers to see if they needed anything. They were okay and busy tallying up the results on a little adding machine.

Florida state law required election officials to post

the results on the polling place door. A small piece of clear tape attached to a small printout fulfilled the law.

Pastor Martin read the results—75 % to 25%, the ultra-conservative candidate won in a landslide. At that moment, the pastor had a sorrowful revelation: The "mid-ground flock" he once served had flown away. Though he continued to love the people, he concluded that they would need a new shepherd, and he would have to retire early.

I find it curious that taxonomists use different names to distinguish different groupings of birds. For example, a flock of owls is called a "parliament", a flock of pelicans is called a "squadron", and a flock of crows a "murder". My favorite name designates a flock of flamingoes. These odd-billed pink beauties are called a "flamboyance." Imagine that!

Is all that necessary? Really? As much as it might make us chuckle, do we really need different names for different flocks of birds?

Humans can't help putting things into categories and subcategories as we struggle to make sense of such a diverse and complex creation. Different groupings and communities exist throughout. According to the Bible, this is God's doing.

"Then the LORD God said, "It's not good that the human is alone. I will make him a helper that is perfect for him."

Genesis 2: 18 - (Common English Bible)

From the biblical wisdom of the book of Genesis comes the notion that God created a community so the human creature would not be alone. The early pages of the Bible describe and identify families and tribes as the primary communal groups.

In the pre-history, mythic time of Noah, many tribes and family groups populated the earth. Instead of God's intended harmony, these groups fought and defiled creation with violence (see Genesis 6:5-13). God decided to start over again and chose Noah's family because Noah was good and righteous. And so the flood story seeks to reset creation. Afterward, using a rainbow in the sky, God promises never to destroy the earth again. Noah's children set out to repopulate human communities.

The initial creation stories and the Noah re-creation story tell of the common ancestry of humanity and the spread of human tribes from a common starting point. Later, scripture will differentiate these tribes and claim specialness for one of those tribes, the one descended through Abraham, Isaac, and Jacob. Even so, there is a recognition that various tribes exist, interact, fight, make peace, and cooperate. All flocks are linked back to God.

Recall the words cited at the beginning of this chapter from the prophet Isaiah (Isaiah 25:6-9), who imagines a time when divisions heal, and the diversity of the nations is cause for celebration as God wipes the tears from all eyes and removes the shroud of death that hangs over all. All people of every tribe and creed will rest in the One who created them - this is a great joy for all the world!

In the meantime, amid tribal divisions, alliances, affinities, and animosities, the flock that follows Jesus has a role to play. Jesus's life, death, and resurrection give us a visionary foretaste of God's future. Moreover, the stories about Jesus's life and teachings provide us with core values to participate in the coming of God's dream for all humanity.

Biblical justice is the practical application of God's love for all as it seeks to address the brokenness, greed, and inequities that have plagued humankind since the days of Noah. The tradition of caring for those who are poor, disadvantaged, and marginalized goes back to scriptural law and prophets. Moses commanded that even those of questionable legal status, such as resident aliens, widows, and orphans, be honored and not oppressed: "You shall not wrong or oppress a resident alien, for you were aliens in the land of Egypt. You shall not abuse any widow or orphan (Exodus 22:21-22)."

Biblical justice involves a tangible leveling of the rough and rocky playing field that privileges and prejudices certain tribes above others. It is often messy political work, but it does not belong to any partisan camp. People of various faiths must debate and discern to apply values that benefit all. Cooperation and collaboration are necessary to bring about biblical justice.

Unfortunately, we live in a culture where radical individualism and commercialism take a different direction than seeking God and God's dream for all. Self-interest fuels our concerns, drives partisanship, lessens collaboration, and inflames insecurity and fear. Sin—that inescapable separation from God— permeates the "me-first" thinking of our times and scatters God's flock.

What to do?

Although we might be tempted to do nothing when overwhelmed by the extent of the problem, that would be a mistake. We may not have the power and agency to change our society and culture solely by promoting biblical justice. Even so, we each have the influence and abilities to make significant inroads among those we encounter.

By sharing our time, talents, and treasure, we can bear witness to an alternative set of values based on Jesus's teaching. Instead of hate, we can choose love. Instead of apathy, we can empathize with others' struggles and pains. Instead of hoarding, we can share. We can also repent.

Repentance is a turning toward God's way and teaching. Instead of following those who fly on the wings of greed and consumption, we can follow in the formation of love as we seek biblical justice for all. We can mount up with the wings of eagles and follow Jesus's lead, soaring into the joyful promise of God's future.

Across the whole earth,
God's love takes flight upon wings,
among different flocks:
giving lift to those who hurt;
carrying hope to us all.

———————————

Let's return to the imaginative next chapter of Jesus's parable of the Good Samaritan. What does the victim, who was Jewish and abandoned by members of his own flock, do when he realizes that a Samaritan rescued him? How might he have coped with the truth about who saved his life? What new conclusions might he make about those outside his flock?

As morning breaks and the sun's golden rays stream through the dust of the small room in the roadside inn, strength rapidly returns to the one the robbers left for dead on the side of the road. Might these have been his thoughts?

It is a beautiful sight to see the sunrise on another day! I thought my days of life were over on that road as I lost consciousness after the second of my fellow believers ignored me. I was a sure goner. Maybe that is why they left me alone. Perhaps they saw that I had no hope of recovery.

Although my body continues to ache, the pain comes with an assurance that I'm still alive. I feel because I continue to be. And I continue to be because another refused to pass by without stopping to help.

By the time my rescuer arrived, I was hardly aware. I couldn't make out his face, and he blurred into the rugged terrain's background. Kindness brought water to my parched lips. I lapped the refreshing liquid with frantic abandon, then faded away into the embrace of the one God sent my way.

The next thing I remember is waking up in this bed with clean bandages covering my head, hands, and chest.

I asked the innkeeper's wife about my savior's identity. "A nice man took care of you; he paid us up front to meet your needs," she replied.

Other than this faint description, I had no further details about the mystery man.

I owe him a lot. I will sing his praise in the synagogue when I finally have the strength to go home. With increased strength every day, it won't be long before I will reunite with my family. They must be sick with worry.

The door creaks open. A figure walks into the room. Standing in the rays of sunshine, he has an aura like some heavenly being. It is my angel, the one who saved my life. Stepping closer, I see his face for the first time.

Something is wrong. He is not a Jew but a Samaritan. Samaritans are half-blooded people who worship God in the wrong way. Ever since childhood, everyone warned me about the likes of them. Has he come to rob me?

What I heard next changed my life, challenging every bias I held. The Samaritan spoke to me in a gentle tone, "I'm glad to see that you are up. Have they been taking good care of you?"

Joy blossoms within me as a new realization takes hold. God's presence and love extend beyond my tribe. The flock that follows God's teaching is bigger than I thought. According to God's way, even Samaritans and Jews care for each other. Praise Adonai!

A conversation with a non-profit worker from a local relief organization that assists the unhoused and poor population in Southwest Florida inspired the following fictional story.

For ten years, Joe volunteered twice weekly to drive the bus. It didn't matter that he didn't have a commercial driver's license because the bus was small enough. Anyone with a regular driver's license could drive, even former executives of Fortune 500 companies.

Joe got up before sunrise on his scheduled days to begin his route. He would drive through the extended neighborhood, picking up the passengers headed to a food distribution pavilion in a local park.

Usually, those who boarded the bus did so with multiple children in tow. They were madres (mothers) caring for their children who are not old enough to attend school. The padres (fathers) work long, hard hours as day laborers in the fields or landscaping. Some have papers, and some don't.

Many wait at the local gas station until a stranger picks them up for a job. The system is rife with exploitation and danger. So many things can go wrong, and sometimes they do. The Madres carry on with their children, thankful for any help and kindness they can get through life's challenges.

As each enters the small bus, they greet the driver. Joe responds with his limited Spanish vocabulary, "Buenos Dias." The two languages struggle as each tries to understand the other, and much of what both say gets lost in translation. However, the kindness comes through, blessing the driver and his passengers.

Most days, Joe's bus is full when he arrives at his destination. More volunteers, who also get up early, greet his passengers as they disembark. These dedicated and joyful folks prepare tables of garage sale items, diapers, other baby essentials, fresh vegetables and fruits, and a hot meal. It is all free for the taking.

Some volunteers speak a little Spanish, but most do not. Smiles and laughter break the language barrier. Joy increases as bags fill with food, supplies, and household items. The pavilion provides needed essentials to ease the strain on these struggling families.

It also provides meaning and purpose to those whose lives contain many things. Many of these volunteers are the proverbial "Snowbirds" who migrate south during winter to escape the cold. They retired or semi-retired from years of hard work and now come to Florida to enjoy the benefits of their labor. Their full schedules include many activities such as golf, pickleball, bike riding, eating out, walking along the beach, watching the sunset, and volunteering to help others.

If you ask them why they come to the park, many say they want to give back, help the less fortunate, and love their neighbor. Those with a faith perspective might link their actions with Jesus's compassionate teachings, and others who aren't religious would agree it is the right thing to do.

Folks of different partisan persuasions suspend divisive politics as they cooperate for the common good, holding judgments, certainties, and ideologies. When they are under the roof of the park pavilion, they have a common purpose - to care for those who come in need.

Their generosity of time, money, and spirit generates priceless joy. They find meaning and purpose in their lives as they open their hearts and hands to help their fellow humans. They discover what Jesus's followers have known for generations: joy comes through engagement and service.

Joe knows this to the bottom of his being. He is full of joy each time he picks up a new passenger and, in broken Spanish, says, "Buenos Dias."

———————————

Sitting on my beach chair on the sand, I watch a squadron of pelicans fly inches above the water in an elegant formation. They swiftly and quietly complete their aerial survey, heading to their nesting place.

Earlier in the day, I watched them dive headfirst into the water, fishing. From a fair height above the waves, they plummet. Splash! They emerge, shaking their feathers, often without a fish. Now and then, they get lucky. They snap their elongated beaks and swallow their aquatic prey.

My reflection on the pelican's precision flight is interrupted as I look at the oscillating surf. Back and forth, the waves advance and recede. As the water moves, so do the Sandpipers. Back and forth, their little legs scurry. Their feathered bodies follow the surf, avoiding getting wet and expending so much energy. I get tired just watching their anxious efforts. Here comes the wave; there go the birds. There goes the wave; here comes the birds. Whew!

These flocks live together in the same space. Instead of interfering, these birds carried out their survival tasks side by side.

Without the fish and clams produced by their efforts, they would no longer be around. Within their movements lies a pattern of life. These avian communities are part of the dance of creation.

We might learn something from the birds. Different species coexist side by side. And it is not just them. Within the same general area are Spoonbills, Glossy Ibis, White Ibis, Snowy Egrets, Great Blue Herons, Wood storks, vultures, etc. They fly separately and together in the same sky. Diversity and difference come together as part of the created order.

It is not a perfect example. You might point out that some birds, like humans, raid the nests of others.

Raptors can swoop down and hunt smaller birds with razor-sharp talons. That is all true. But as I sit on the beach and watch, I am inspired by those who fly in flocks upon the same wind without incident. We could use more of that in the human world.

Instead of seeing our differences and diversity as something to fear, exploit, or ignore, what if we flapped proverbial wings in the direction of God's dream, espoused in Isaiah's vision of all nations coming together in God's presence?

What if instead of domination, exclusion, and condemnation, we applied some of the teachings of Jesus regarding love and acceptance? What if we formed communities where compassion drove action that brought people together, provided for their needs, respected their dignity, and celebrated their uniqueness? What if we applied biblical justice?

Following Jesus and sharing in God's love for all will bring unexpected joy, like the seventy individuals Jesus sent out to carry on his work in the towns ahead of him. They were to enter communities and bring God's peace. Where places welcomed their efforts, amazing things happened.

According to Luke's Gospel, "The seventy returned with joy, saying, "Lord, in your name even the demons submit to us! (Luke 10:17)." The gospel changed lives.

Diversity prevailed over divisions. Fellowship bridged isolation. Healing soothed brokenness. Where places didn't welcome them, they moved on, not seeking revenge or violence. They simply flew away to another location.

Flocking together, they enlarged the flock of God. This exciting work made them all full of joy.

CHAPTER FOUR: SHELLS & DRIFTWOOD

"...what woman having ten silver coins, if she loses one of them, does not light a lamp, sweep the house, and search carefully until she finds it? When she has found it, she calls together her friends and neighbors, saying, 'Rejoice with me, for I have found the coin that I had lost.'"

Luke 15: 8-9

Walking barefoot in the receding foam of the surf, I look intently at the sand. There are dozens of tiny bubbles rising from small indentations. Retreating crustaceans make these holes as they dive deep into the wet sand as the water returns to the Gulf. These are the hunting grounds of the Sandpipers and other shorebirds who peck at shells for food.

Floridian beaches are known for their shells, and this reputation is well-earned. This novice beachcomber has been satisfied with the availability, variety, and color of the shells that lie open in the beach drift. These are ocean gems to find and behold.

Though they were once a living creature's protective cover, the shells are usually empty and cleaned when the waves wash them upon the shore. When we pick up these lifeless remnants, they shift from being the former homes for marine life to being treasures in our homes.

In addition to shells, when you walk upon the moist sand between the waterline and the strandline, you see other things that have washed up, such as driftwood and sea glass. These discarded, forgotten, lost, and abandoned items were adrift on the tide and altered by the elements and salty sea. Some items are now smooth or bleached due to lengthy exposure.

I wonder about its origin when I hold one of these washed-up treasures. Whence did this shell, driftwood, or piece of sea glass come? If it could speak, what story would it tell?

What was it like when it was alive on the ocean floor, filtering out microscopic sustenance as the tide oscillated?

Where was this small branch, and from what kind of tree did it break off? Did a storm cause the breakage, or was it simply a part of the natural arboreal living and dying process?

And that tiny piece of glass smoothed safe by the sea, what was that from? Did the bottle fall overboard at some party on a dock somewhere? Was someone out fishing and got careless, or did they purposely toss the empty overboard? Was it the result of a shipwreck?

If only these things could speak. But they can't. These remnants upon the beach are forever silent.

There is sadness in hidden stories. It is even more so when those stories belong to people who are discarded, abandoned, and adrift upon life's tumultuous seas. The joy of those who suffer alone can be as empty as the shells on the beach. Those who find themselves broken away from family and friends can be as dry and lifeless as driftwood.

As a Floridian bartender told me, "We have the same problems in paradise as anywhere else, just warmer." As a pastor, I have noticed that loneliness is one of these significant problems.

People move to Florida for various reasons, including retirement, the nice weather, jobs, opportunities, and freedom from injustice in their homeland. When they do, they often leave family elsewhere. They also leave behind their communities of origin, where they are known and have history.

After moving, they make new friends and acquaintances. Some take up a sport like golf or pickleball. Life is good (or at least better than it was) for a time. They live the proverbial "dream."

But life changes, and things move on. Circumstances shift, and the state's transient nature catches up. With most of their family living elsewhere, they must travel to keep in touch. When that travel becomes strained and infrequent, visits are limited to once or twice a year. Families lose touch and are less of a physical support.

Emptiness and loneliness sneak in and linger. They harp on the past and what might have been. These emotions no longer welcome the future and its potential. Stuck in the present, they suffer alone. At this point, joy is usually not a sustaining part of the picture.

Spiritually, we can feel disconnected when we are apart from others. Isolated and lonely, we might feel that God is also distant. When this happens, we suffer double.

Alone, without a friend or helper, it is a defeating prospect, full of despair. Anger, fear, and resignation can seem overwhelming. We might want to give up or crawl into hiding. The temptation to turn inward is real and only exasperates the situation of our separation.

When you hear "sin," different things might come to mind. For many, sin is a moral deficiency, something you say or do wrong. We have hurt someone or violated some golden rule that upsets what is good in life. We make others mad, including God, when our actions go bad. In the case of such sin, we require forgiveness. There is a need for restitution, including a heartfelt apology.

We can also think of sin in terms of separation. Often, we can find ourselves a distance from others. A gap exists between us. Somehow, something has broken our relationship. At times, we can make amends. Other times, try as we might, we cannot repair the breach. Over time, the chasm increases. Separated, we suffer by ourselves.

No matter how we define sin, whether in terms of morality or separation, it is a joyless proposition. We might chuckle and even enjoy certain depravities, but that is not joy. Laughing at the expense of another, for example, lacks the essence of genuine joyfulness, which comes from being in a right and loving relationship with another.

Where love is absent, and we are apart from God and others, joy gets missed. Again, we might feel pleasure and happiness, but that spiritual condition of joy that holds meaning and purpose, allowing us to rejoice from the depths of our being, is wanting.

This chapter examines loneliness, suffering, and forgiveness in our search for joy, God, and paradise. We will find that joy is not reserved for those moments when the sun shines, and everything goes our way. Joy comes even amid sorrow and when we feel washed up on life's proverbial shoreline.

Walking on the soft, wet shoreline, feeling the water gently cover my toes, I look for shells. The Gulf Shore beaches are a trove of them, but it takes patience and diligence to find something that is a keeper. Carefully, my eyes scan the sand, searching.

My biblical imagination kicks into gear. What must the woman in Jesus's beloved parable have felt as she searched for her lost coin? Might her thoughts have gone something like this?

Now, where did I put that blasted coin? A poor woman should know where her limited resources are. It is not like I have thousands of coins to handle. Ten coins is all I have, had. 10% of my wealth is now gone.

For twenty years, I managed to survive as a widow. I kept my house clean, sweeping the floor regularly. I used coins sparingly, replenishing my treasury by doing odd jobs.

Being frugal, I didn't need much, so I didn't spend much.

Somehow, however, I let my guard down. Where is that coin? Careless, careless - I've been so reckless. Is this the start of my decline? How long will it be until I lose the rest of the coins?

Maybe I didn't lose them. Did someone break in and steal my coin? Why take only one? Did I leave it out unguarded on the table? Was the temptation too great for one of my neighbors to take advantage of a widow? Perhaps it was one of those kids! There are too many children running around these days. The noise of their chatter can irritate me to no end.

I must sit down and think. Where was I last? When did I last have all my coins together?

For the life of me, I can't recall when I last had things together. When was life complete? It has been a long time since I felt whole. Widows are both ignored and avoided in most circles. Do I even have a circle these days?

I feel like a piece of dried-up wood that washes ashore on the Galilean beach. What good am I? I can't even keep track of ten coins. I feel helpless.

The story will continue...

———————

The following true story comes from a friend who has tended many Floridian Tiki bars. It happened a few years ago in the Florida Keys.

It was near closing time when the guy came into the bar. He appeared agitated, raising concern. My bartender friend, James, was alone.

Excitedly speaking in Spanish made it hard for James to understand him even though he was fluent. With hands waving and pointing outside, the questionable customer repeated, "Ese es mi barco! Ese es mi barco!"

Helping to create an eclectic and exotic atmosphere for thirsty tourists, the Tiki Bar's owner collected various items of interest. An old 4x4, assorted antiques, tin signs, and countless items littered inside and outside the dried palm-branched roofed building that housed the bar. The unique collection was constantly growing.

When a new artifact of interest became available, the owner occasionally sent his employees on procurement missions. On one such assignment, my friend James secured an old boat from a marina going out of business. It was a rundown wooden craft whose sea-worthy days, if ever there were such days, were in the distant past. The broken boat made a perfect addition to the tiki collection.

"That's my boat!" The man asserted in English as he pointed his finger outside toward the newly acquired treasure. Trying to calm him down, my friend was more worried than ever. Did the marina steal the boat from this poor man? Was it lost in a poker game by this drunken gambler? What did it matter? That boat couldn't float! Would this guy become violent as he tried to reclaim his alleged property?

Leaning on his experience dealing with unruly (and often drunken) customers, James overcame his anxiety and tried to calm him down. Offering a pint glass of water, my friend talked calmly and reassuringly, "Tell me about it; how is it your boat?"

After downing the water, the middle-aged Hispanic fellow cooled down. "I will come back tomorrow to show you." With that, he left the tiki bar.

Thinking the whole encounter was strange, James closed up the bar for the night, not expecting to see that troubled soul again.

Imagine his surprise the next day when James saw the stranger return with an old photo album tucked under his arm. Adolfo carefully opened the yellow-paged book. Behind the aged plastic film was a collection of fading Polaroid pictures taken two decades before. "That is my boat!" He pointed to a picture, then pointed outside. The story unfolded.

Ten years ago, in 2012, during the days of the "wet feet, dry feet" immigration policy, any Cuban caught on the waters between Cuba and the United States (with "wet feet") would be turned back, while those who made it to shore ("dry feet") would be allowed to stay in the United States and qualified for expedited legal status per the 1966 Cuban Adjustment Act.

Along with eleven others, Adolfo left his native island in a boat they built. Materials for their marine vessel included old boards from the family barn and an engine appropriated from a Police car. It was makeshift at best, but it carried nine passengers through the cover of darkness to freedom's shore. Tragically, three Cubans didn't survive the treacherous journey. With "dry feet," Adolfo joined the company of hardworking immigrants who became citizens. He was the only one in his band of fleeing refugees to do so successfully.

The plight of refugees continues to be a part of the story of the land we call "paradise." Though policies and attitudes change, sometimes violently and abruptly, those who flee their native land do so at significant risk. Willingly, they set themself adrift on the waves of luck, which remain fickle and harsh.

Immigration remains a sensitive issue in the divided political environment of "paradise." What do we do with the onslaught of those who come across our southern border? Fear permeates perceptions and has stymied productive solutions.

Yet, one cannot deny the presence of migrants and immigrants (both legal and illegal), as they make up a significant portion of the backbone of the paradise economy's service and agricultural sectors. From washing dishes and making beds to picking tomatoes and strawberries, we may overlook or deny their struggle. Still, their toil remains essential to business, agriculture, and tourism.

Imagine Adolfo's surprise when he was driving home after a long day of work under the Florida sun and saw his barco! Gratitude and joy overwhelmed and disoriented him as he entered the tiki bar the night before.

There were too many words to say: struggle, sacrifice, oppression, escape, fear, desperation, hope. These powerful emotions and more washed ashore as the former refugee reunited with the hull of the rough barn boards that brought him to his new home.

Even though bartenders are rarely lost for words, James was speechless. Instead, he simply reached out and grabbed Adolfo's hand in a gesture of friendship. The men shared a genuine moment of joy.

My walk along the beach continues. Occasionally, I step on a submerged shell, which causes discomfort. Life can contain many hidden challenges and trials. The theologian in me starts pondering the human struggle and how loneliness complicates matters. Further, what role do sin and separation from God play?

Loneliness and forgiveness are not usually connected. After all, it is often no one's fault that we are alone. What have we done wrong to warrant forgiveness?

But if we define sinning as a separation or brokenness in relationships, we may connect the dots between loneliness and forgiveness and uncover a pathway toward healing and joy.

The challenge that lonely people face is much the same as the sorrowful sinner faces. How do you repair life's brokenness? It is not like we have access to a super glue that can fix shattered promises and hurts. We don't. You also can't quickly restore trust. Sometimes, it is impossible to pay restitution and make amends. We are stuck.

Thankfully, God is not stuck.

Forgiveness flows from God's steadfast, abundant, and eternal love. It is unearned and has more to do with God's graceful nature than anything we can do, achieve, acquire, or aspire to.

Since we all find ourselves separated from God and broken in our relationships, we cannot effect the transformation needed to pull ourselves out of the muck and restore ourselves to a joyful and meaningful life.

If left to our devices, we would be alone and without hope. Thankfully, Jesus's life teaches us about the nearness of God's reign. Moreover, God desires a compassionate connection with all creation. God's love seeks us out in our sin and separation. By God's grace, we are not alone.

Forgiveness happens as God embraces us with love that refuses to let us go. God restores us into a relationship that produces joy. We are blessed to live and grow into our identity as God's beloved children.

Forgiveness is future-oriented. Healthy relationships constantly need renewal and the restorative power that comes from the willingness to move on beyond the hurt of the past. That doesn't mean that the hurt magically disappears; it doesn't. However, it suggests that we won't stop loving even as we hurt and that our love looks to the next chapter of our relationship.

Forgiveness has a communal dimension that we would do well to remember. God's love connects us to God and establishes and binds our relationships in love with others, including family, friends, and strangers.

The vertical nature of our loving relationship with God intersects with our horizontal relationship with others. The reality of Divinely inspired connections replaces loneliness and all its heartaches with new possibilities. No longer does our past dictate or limit our future.

It is not to say that overnight forgiveness makes all the lonely and the hurt disappear. Though such miraculous experiences occur from time to time, it is more likely that we will need to be intentional in our work. We need patience in ourselves and others as we make cautious movements, sometimes baby steps, moving ever so slightly forward. Trust and relationships take time to reestablish and build.

Where there is loss and loneliness, the gospel of Jesus Christ comes as a gift full of potential joy. It reestablishes our central relationship with our Creator. We find that we are beloved and connected with God. No matter what we've done or not done, God restores us into communion with Christ.

From that place, the love that drives forgiveness pushes us beyond ourselves to interact with others. Love seeks an ever-widening community. Loneliness dissipates as our lives link with others.

Though it takes time, God's powerful love and grace, which knows no bounds, seeks to transform even the most desperate cases. God finds the empty-most parts of our being and loves us into newness. A future different from a simple projection of the past emerges. Joy bursts forth, and it compels us to join in the celebration.

The theological reflections of this amateur beachcomber lead me back to thinking about that woman who lost her coin. Again, trying to imagine her struggle, I get lost in my thoughts. In her frantic search, might she have thought something like this?

I am tired. This search has consumed all my energy and produced nothing. I have swept every corner of my small living space without success.

I am beginning to think that I'm losing my mind. How could I lose something so valuable?

Perhaps I should call it quits and accept that my coin is gone forever. It wouldn't be the first time in my life that I suffered a loss. Lord knows that I've grieved plenty.

Each loss brings up all the previous ones. As a widow, I am still not over the loss of my husband. When he died, it felt like a part of me died as well. Many days, there is an emptiness inside that I can't seem to fill.

Wait a minute! It is coming back to me. The other day, when I went to the market, I was wearing my apron with the pocket. Did I have my coin with me? Think. Think. Yes.

I was going to use it to buy some flour, but I ran into my friend. She gave me some of her flour as she had an extra measure. How could I forget her kindness?

I must check the front pocket of my apron that hangs on that peg across the room.

Sure enough; praise the Lord! It was in my apron! I am overjoyed to have found my coin. It wasn't lost but misplaced.

Loneliness and grief blinded me in my haste and panic. Negative energy, including an unhealthy dose of self-pity, consumed me. In the process, I forgot that I had others who loved and cared for me. I might live by myself, but I am not alone in this world. Neighbors look in on me like the one who gave me the flour.

Although I am a widow, and that is not an easy thing to be, some pray for me, include me, and share generously with me. Their Christian kindness comes from their faith in a God who is compassionate and concerned with the outcasts, downtrodden, orphans, and even widows. Following the teachings of Jesus, they put their faith into tangible practice.

Holding my treasure in my hand, I feel a new joy. I know what I will do. I will take this coin and make it an offering of thanksgiving. I will host a party. I will share my newly found joy with others.

———————

My toe bumps into something hard, partially buried. Using my foot as a rake, I move the wet sand away to reveal a colorful Calico Scallop. It is a beautiful shell with rusty ridges. Although it is a little worn, it is a keeper.

As I wash away the remaining sand from the shell, I resolve to use it as an ornament on my tropical Christmas tree next year. We put an artificial holiday tree on our lanai, decorated with shells. It is our "Florida" tree.

Putting the Calico Scallop into my pocket, I am curious whence it came. Like the community I serve as pastor, the shell comes from somewhere else. Consider this typical story...

About ten years ago, Fred and Darlene decided that the winters were getting colder and longer. They no longer wanted to shovel the snow and feared slipping on the ice. Although they were born and raised in Upstate New York, now that they were retired—he from insurance, she from teaching—they yearned for a warmer clime.

So, they joined the snowbirds' annual migration to the Sunshine State. At first, Fred and Darlene rented a condo for a month to escape the bitter cold in January. When the Christmas holidays ended, they drove south on Highway 95.

After a few years of renting, they wanted to own a slice of paradise. At that point, they expanded their stay from January through April. Life was good as long as they made it home for Darlene to make Easter dinner for the extended family.

Fred and Darlene's family supported their "snowbirding" with multiple visits. It was joyous to host each of their children as they brought their growing families on vacation. The condo wasn't giant, but it could accommodate the grandkids, who loved seeing Grandma and Grandpa in Florida. There were walks on the beach, local attractions, and trips for ice cream.

For almost a decade, the pattern repeated itself annually. Joy filled Fred and Darlene. For them, "snowbirding" in Florida was the best of all worlds. They enjoyed being with family up north in the summer and on holidays. Happiness continued down south in the winter. Sun shone across the seasons in their lives. Endless summer seemed to shine endlessly.

Yet, life is constantly changing. Grandkids grow up and have families of their own. Job changes move middle-aged children across the country. Maintaining two houses is complicated and increasingly expensive. Each year, Darlene sets fewer place settings around her holiday table. Driving thousands of miles in winter and spring gets harder.

One day, Fred and Darlene decided, for various reasons, that it was time to move to Florida full-time. Now experienced retirees, they wanted to play more golf and pickleball. So they sold their home of fifty years and bought a larger place in Southwest Florida.

Their schedule was busy. In addition to their sporting interests, activities at their homeowner's association, occasional cruises out of Miami, and dining out, they became associate members of a local church. They made new friends who had also drifted upon the same proverbial tide.

After church, for example, they talked with the woman who always sat in the row directly in front of them. She also happened to be from New York. They invited her to brunch with them, establishing a weekly habit. Each Sunday, they worshiped with Ruth and then ate with her at a local dinner.

Somewhere around July, Darlene began to fret about the advancing holidays. What would they do for Christmas? Their kids and grandkids lived in four states and already had multiple plans. She could take part in any one of their celebrations. A few of the super planners had already extended invitations. But how could she choose? Besides, it was a lot of traveling.

After much discussion, Fred and Darlene decided to stay put. They would spend their first Christmas in Florida, another adventure in a series of novelty experiences in their new chapter of life.

As Fall came, things seemed strange. The weather didn't get colder, and the leaves didn't change color. Fred kept mowing the lawn in November.

Thanksgiving came abruptly. Darlene made a small turkey and smaller portions of all her famous sides. It was a feast by any definition. Yet, something was missing. They were alone.

For the first time in their lives, they dreaded the approaching Yuletide. Why did they leave everything behind and move to a place where the weather was "perfect" year-round? Although they cursed the snow and ice in the past, now they longed for flurries and frost. Talking to their kids only made them more homesick.

Decorating the palm tree in the front yard while wearing shorts was a bizarre experience for Fred. His memories of having frozen fingers while hanging lights became golden nostalgia. Darlene's Christmas cookies didn't turn out right. Her time-tested recipes didn't seem to work right in the Florida heat. The butter wouldn't stay cold enough.

Awkward. Strange. Alone.

On the First Sunday of Advent, after the closing hymn, Ruth turned around and kindly asked, "What are your plans for Christmas?" Darlene responded less than enthusiastically, "We are staying home." Fred interrupted, "Our first Christmas in fifty years with just the two of us."

"Would you like to join me for Christmas dinner? I'll have a few folks over, and it would be great if you could join us," Ruth invited her new friends.

Fred looked at Darlene. She instantaneously returned his affectionate glance. Smiling, Darlene and Fred readily accepted the gracious offer. They were not going to be alone after all. They found a place and a joy to celebrate.

I return to my beach chair, moving away from the waves crashing upon the shore. I deposited the results of my beachcombing into a small pile. There are a few welks, scallop shells, and bits of smooth wood. I will take most of these finds home and add them to my growing collection.

Today, the surf is unusually rough. Though I can't always see it, each wave brings things to bestow upon the sand. The oscillating tide transports everything from microscopic algae to driftwood, shells, and other sea life. Each item comes dislocated from elsewhere.

Each item's past has closed as they lie on the beach unprotected from the sun's scorching rays; their present reality is dry and lifeless. Loneliness, isolation, emptiness, and a sense of loss are emotions we can easily project upon these remnants of the sea.

At some point in our lives, maybe even now, we experience the feeling of being washed up and dried out, like partial bits of shells and driftwood, mere remnants of our past selves. This is not a good feeling, especially when it persists and lingers.

Often, a sense of isolation and loneliness accompanies us as uninvited and unwanted companions on a scary, dark road.

It is easy to question our worth and purpose in such circumstances. Looking in the mirror, we may not like what we see. We might judge harshly: worthless, stupid, helpless, and unlovable. When we start believing these horrible lies that we tell about ourselves, we can slip into a depressed state. There might even be a need for us to seek medical attention.

Since life's many ups and downs bear a constant need to reconnect with God and others, let me suggest that we could all use a bit of spiritual restoration. No matter where we find ourselves today, we could use the refreshment of God's love and care.

Thankfully, like the constant roll of the waves that transport all sorts of items upon the shore, the continual movement of God's grace washes love upon us. This love comes in various bits and pieces. Sometimes, it is complete and unquestionable, readily identifiable. Other times, we might not even recognize it. Still, it might be hard and buried, discovered when we step on it.

Though varied in shape, substance, color, and recognizability, God's love comes to us without conditions or exclusions, in abundance, and has the potential to transform.

God's compassion and forgiveness break through loneliness by creating connections with God and others, opening an unimaginable future. Beloved by God, we find love's purpose and opportunities to love others. Relationships form, rebuild, refocus, and continue. We understand anew that we are not alone in this world, even if we live by ourselves.

As these new perceptions and perspectives settle in, there is cause for celebration. Filled with joy, we can't help ourselves. Suddenly, we need to share generously and enthusiastically what we have found. God is near, and God is good. Yay!

CHAPTER FIVE: PALM TREES

"The righteous flourish like the palm tree and grow like a cedar in Lebanon. They are planted in the house of the LORD; they flourish in the courts of our God. In old age they still produce fruit; they are always green and full of sap, showing that the LORD is upright; he is my rock, and there is no unrighteousness in him."

Psalm 92:12-15

You see them almost everywhere that you look. Palm trees are abundant in Florida, and the variety is a horticulturist's dream. A short walk around the manicured streets in my neighborhood reveals more palms than you could count on fingers and toes.

You find Paurotis Palms, Florida Silver Palms, and Cabbage Palms—all native to the state. Cataract Palms from Mexico, European Fan Palms from the Mediterranean coast, Christmas Palms from the Philippines, Carpentaria Palms from Australia, Coconut Palms from Southeast Asia, and Bismarck Palms from Madagascar - they come from far away places. Because of the tropical climate, almost all the 2,500 palm species worldwide can and do grow here.

There is something regal about a tall branchless trunk with a crown of green fronds on top. Maybe the sentiment goes back to my childhood Palm Sunday celebrations, but these exotic trees have always held a sense of majesty for me. I remember how thrilled I was to get a piece of palm in worship. We used it to make a cross, which I then put on the wall in my bedroom. Imagine my delight as I now go to the back end of the church's property to cut down fresh palm branches for Palm Sunday worship.

The image of a hammock strung between two slanted palm trees is iconic. Under the shade of the palm trees, we find a relaxing paradise or at least the cover of a Jimmy Buffet album.

This chapter will use palm trees as a guiding image. What does it mean to rest in the shelter of God? What shelters us in life? How do we provide shelter for ourselves and others?

We will also examine reconciliation's role in our relationships with others. Along with God's values of forgiveness, grace, and mercy, reconciliation is essential for reestablishing a secure place to rest connected with others and God. It is critical because our relationships are bound to strain and sometimes break. When they do, trust can be compromised. Without trust, it is impossible to continue.

Reconciliation is not easy. It will take all the wisdom, courage, and selfless love that we can muster. We must move beyond instincts, the "common sense" of our culture, bruised egos, and an assortment of fractured feelings. Following Jesus's teaching of radical love is challenging when lofty theory meets hard reality.

Working towards reconciliation is difficult work for a peacemaker in a war zone. Violence escalates without much effort, and cycles of retribution quickly and exponentially grow. Wastelands and those areas labeled "no man's land" expand and offer no refuge for life. Conflicts continue without much encouragement on micro and macro scales and spiral downward.

Without peaceful intervention, there will be no end to the destruction and eventual retaliation. "Amends" must be made for dignity, cooperation, collaboration, and a positive future to emerge.

Whew! In a time of divisions and conflicts, personal and global, we have our work cut out for us. So, Let us find a shady spot under a palm tree and ponder trust, faith, shelter, and where we feel at home. Resting, aided by deep breaths, we continue our sacred journey of seeking God down the path of reconciliation.

The first time I saw it, it looked strange. I was driving down the local "almost interstate" when I noticed a landscaper in front of me hauling a giant palm tree in the open back of his truck. It was huge and had a massive crown of palm leaves waving in the wind. How did that large tree even fit in that truck? The roots must have been gigantic. It didn't seem possible, like an unrealistic drawing of an enthusiastic child.

Since that day, watching palms transported is not uncommon. Florida's unending development involves adding more of the iconic symbol of paradise. Many people, including me, want to be under the mesmerizing sway of a palm, so the trees are transported in and strategically planted.

Palm trees are different from the deciduous trees that grow up north. Not only do they not change their colors and lose all their leaves seasonally, but the root systems are remarkably distinct. The roots of palms generally do not spread out as the tree grows taller as northern contemporaries do. This feature allows larger palms to be transported and transplanted more easily than you could with comparable-sized deciduous trees.

When Jesus told the parable of the Prodigal Son, he might have been under a palm tree. If he was, that tree was most likely a local variety, unlike the palms in Florida. Folks didn't move around like they do today. Long-lasting family roots and ties provided shelter across generations.

The desire for a son to request his inheritance before his father died was an affront to tightly knitted family groups. Leaving and squandering wealth in a foreign land would receive harsh judgment from the crowd. Why would you leave the shelter of your home and family only to waste it away? Only a fool would do such things.

Jesus's parable does more than highlight the foolishness of a younger son who misuses his opportunities and finds himself outside his family's shelter. It offers a glimpse into God's heart, where forgiveness and grace form the basis for the reconciliation needed to reestablish shelter.

I wonder what it might have been like to be in the household of Jesus' beloved parable of the Forgiving Father and the Prodigal Son and watch the drama unfold. What might have gone through the mind of a trusted household servant? It might have been something like this...

I will never forget that day. The sun burned down without mercy. I rested momentarily in the warm shadow cast by the residence. Already, sweat soaked my clothes, and the day was not half over.

No matter my energy level, I always do my job enthusiastically. It is my role as a household servant. Besides, I never wanted to be a burden. Especially in those days, my master had been through enough that he didn't need drama from me. I can't begin to imagine the anguish that he went through.

If you ask me, he didn't deserve any of it. You would never find a more likable man with a bigger heart if you looked all over Galilee. He remains so kind and generous.

The master treats everyone with compassion, even those who work for him. I can't count all the times he has asked me about my family. When my mother fell sick years ago, he gave me the time off and a few shekels for medicine. After she got better, he seemed as happy as I was in the good fortune. I've never seen anything like it. In this Roman world, folks of his stature don't pay any attention to my kind except to demean, dominate, and take advantage.
What the younger son did to him is just not right. That ingrate!

I can tell you everything his father gave him, and I wouldn't have enough hours in the day. That boy left with his inheritance, half the fortune, treating his father as though he had died, leaving him heartbroken. If that wasn't enough, I've heard he wasted it shamefully. In a short time, he was broke and homeless!

Such disgrace!

Imagine my surprise then in what followed.
I saw a man walking toward the estate with slumped shoulders. He was shabby and unkempt, like another drifter looking for a handout. I had no doubt the master would give him something, maybe even shelter for the night.

Then the shocker came. Someone ran out to meet the stranger—it was the master! The master ran, holding up the hem of his robes so he wouldn't trip. When he reached the transient, the master embraced and kissed him.

I had to get closer to see who would warrant such a welcome.

As I walked toward them, I couldn't believe my eyes. The son, the prodigal, had returned. Instead of anger, his father had greeted him with joy. I was amazed.

The master called my name, interrupting my wonder. He ordered me to start preparations for a feast. I was to stop at no expense. Quickly, I scurried and got started.

The story will continue...

Walking through my neighborhood, you quickly notice all the different varieties of Palm trees. As I mentioned at the start of this chapter, these varieties come from around the world. Some are tall and skinny, others are short and stout. Some trunks are smooth, while others are spikey. Aside from unique characteristics, the various types of Palms seem to grow in clustered groupings or as solitary trees.

As I think about these characteristics of the diverse nature of Palm trees, there are similarities between these plants and us humans. We are certainly a diverse lot from different origins. Some prefer to be left alone, while others naturally congregate.

Further reflection brings a story about a group of college students on a church outing. They are faced with diverse perspectives and the challenge of caring for individuals and the larger community.

They were home from college during the Christmas holiday. Some traveled as far as Texas, Missouri, and Chicago, while others attended school in Florida. These six students received a church-sponsored educational grant. The Scholarship Committee invited them to lunch to celebrate their achievements and learn more about what they were studying.

Their courses of study ranged from physical therapy to construction management, journalism, public medical policy, architecture, and medicine. Although they had different perspectives and personalities, each brought energy and enthusiasm for what they were doing and for the future they were making for themselves. It was inspiring to be in their presence.

A few hours before lunch, Susan, the church's director of faith formation, organized a service opportunity for the students. They all showed up. The task was distributing bags filled with toiletries, socks, candies, and personal items that the church had purchased and put together for the benefit of migrant workers.

Migrant workers contribute to the local economy. They pick crops at harvest and do extensive landscaping work in the hot sun. Some have working papers, and some do not. Many day laborers hang out at gas stations and corners, waiting for a stranger to hire them under the table.

Their money supports their families living nearby in trailer park housing or hundreds of miles away in their homelands. Not only is the work hard, but there is danger and exploitation in the shady underground economy.

On the morning of the scholarship lunch, the college students transported about eighty bags of supplies to a gas station/convenience store parking lot. They arrived around nine o'clock. By that time, all the laborers hired for the day were gone. The remaining laborers would have to try again tomorrow morning.

The employees and volunteers of the Bonita Springs-based community charity clearly instructed the students to hand out only one bag per person. And they did. With compassion and kindness, the students greeted the workers in Spanish. Broken versions of both English and Spanish accompanied the distribution. Gestures and body language filled in the gaps where language failed.

Things proceeded without incident until everyone in the line received a bag. The crowd of unemployed workers received about sixty bags, and twenty were left over. Before they could be loaded back into the truck, one of the recipients returned to the students. He told them about his sick cousin and asked if he could have a bag to take to him.

The student's empathy didn't hesitate. Someone was in need, and they had extra—it seemed an obvious response. However, it started a chain reaction. Suddenly, requests for sick relatives multiplied, and the remaining bags quickly disappeared.

The charity organizers saw what was happening and instantly retrieved the second bag from those who had received it. One per person was the established rule—no exceptions. The one "in charge" said briskly to the students to correct their generosity.

It bothered the students. Why couldn't they? Shouldn't they meet the need before them? Why did there need to be rules about distributing charity?

Even when Susan explained the charity's position of wanting to do the most good with limited resources, the students disagreed. It didn't matter that the extra bags would return to the main distribution center. Within hours, volunteers would hand them out to those who came looking for help. It also didn't matter that giving extra to some when you didn't have extra for all would set up a pattern of inequity in distribution that could incite a mob mentality. These considerations learned by the charity's volunteers through experience didn't satisfy the students.

On the way to the restaurant, the students and Susan discussed the challenges of trying to help those in need. Though it would seem simple enough - give what is needed to those in need - charitable distribution is complex. How does one do the most good in the face of a seemingly endless need and limited resources?

Providing assistance ("shelter") is not easy. Human needs and nature make handing out assistance bags difficult and perplexing. Different perspectives, approaches, and experiences affect and impact how we help others. Wisdom and compassion are required as we follow Jesus's instruction to "feed my sheep (John 21)".

Palm trees have a few features that make them withstand tropical storms with fierce winds. For one, they have many rambling roots that grab onto a lot of soil around the root ball. As long as the soil is dry, this makes for a large anchor, which gives the tree a bottom-heavy base.

Palm trunks are better suited to survive adverse conditions than those of pine or oak trees. Palms don't have the same annual rings as other trees. Instead, imagine a bundle of woody material like wires inside a telephone cable. Palm trunks are incredibly flexible, bending over 40 or 50 degrees.

Last, the leaves of a Palm are well suited for bad weather. The typical tree with multiple branches and leaves captures plenty of sunshine in good conditions. In a storm, however, those branches and leaves serve as a sail, which is easily battered and broken. Palms have no wide-spreading branches, and the leaves fold up, offering less resistance to heavy winds. When wind causes a palm branch to detach, it does so without damage to the rest of the tree[7].

The ability to shelter in bad weather is a critical adaptation for Palm trees in tropical regions susceptible to hurricanes and nasty tropical storms. When the winds kick up, these resilient trees have only one option - ride out the storm. Or not.

Riding out storms, literal and metaphorical, is part of life. Humans aren't always able to evacuate; there are times when we must shelter in place. With all the courage we can muster, we face adversity as best we can.

Our faith is a tremendous resource during these moments that helps us hold on. Faith finds shelter in God's promise and presence.

What a lovely thought... to rest in the shelter of the Most High. It makes me smile to imagine that cozy place in God's protection. What a joy it would be to be safe from all the horrible things that go bump in the night, threaten all that is good, and cause us suffering and pain. Oh, the benefits of believing and trusting in God, my refuge and my fortress. Nothing negative is going to happen to me!

---

[7] For more information about the unique resiliency of palm trees check out plant ecologist Dan Metcalfe's article on the Treehugger.com website.

Unfortunately, such thoughts are usually interrupted. Life happens. And it has been my experience that life isn't always fair. Bad things and times befall good people. Evil is cruel and seems to delight in victimizing the innocent and vulnerable.

In over twenty-five years of pastoral ministry, I have presided over too many funerals of saints who left us all too soon. It angers me when I hear folks blather on about "just believe" or "pray hard enough" and everything will turn out well. Such naivety is best reserved for feel-good movies. To me, such sentiments dishonor the faithful lives of those who suffer and have died untimely deaths. And that makes me mad.

It also concerns me that "just believe/pray hard enough" theology is unbiblical and creates unreasonable expectations about life following Jesus. When I say "unbiblical," it is not that those who profess such prosperity gospels don't use the Bible—they do. But they cherry-pick self-serving passages out of context to put on bumper stickers, emojis, and social-media posts. Without a critical interpretive lens, they reduce scripture's prophetic and transformative voice to whatever serves their predetermined agenda of unrestricted personal happiness.

Not only are the words and phrases of scripture important, but so is the background from which they come. Our Bible, in both testaments, tells not only the story of God but also that of humanity. At points, the Bible can get as messy as human relationships. The struggle is part of the story. Through moments of faith and doubt, triumph and defeat, abundance and injustice, life and death, God's people exist, survive, and thrive.

Scripture opens pathways that lead to balance and biblical justice for all humanity and creation. As such, there are boundaries to love that refocus and redirect individual whims and desires for the common good.

God's steadfast love and faithfulness meet people where they are. God nurtures and inspires souls, giving them strength and courage to face all sorts of calamities and trials. Transformation happens in the encounter and interchange between God's life and humanity's. This is not some hokey magic that casts an impenetrable shield that repulses all evil.

Crosses still happen. Sometimes, the devil and all the forces that defy God seem to prevail. At sundown on Good Friday, all creation moans over the death of a part of the Trinity.

The crying of creation continues as innocents bleed and children die, as injustices dehumanize and denigrate, as pollution and toxins destroy environments, as violence and abuse rage, and as illnesses cripple. Suffering is inescapable, overwhelming, and often beyond our control.

But we aren't the only ones who cry out. On the cross, tears are found in the very eyes of God. The love that holds Jesus to the cross proclaims the good news that God shares solidarity with all the hurts and brokenness of our suffering. God's love descends to the deepest depths of our sorrow from the highest heaven. We are not alone.

It is from this place that we find a different kind of shelter. Beyond platitudes, bumper stickers, and wishful thinking, God accompanies us through the deepest nights and the hottest part of our days. Love provides a shade that protects our fragile spirits.

Mystery and complexity surround our sacred relationship with the Creator. It is not easily explained or dumbed down. Yet, there is a truth about our life with God that is not shaken. It brings courage that endures regardless of circumstances and outcomes.

My heart returns to those saints I spoke above. Their lives, no matter how long or prosperous, bear witness to God and God's undying presence. They rested in God's love through ups and downs, moments of clarity and confusion, doubts and certainty. They trusted and believed even when things didn't go their way. Among hardship and heartaches, they found something you cannot buy, manufacture, or fake. They found the peace that comes from being connected to God and others.

Here is where the psalmist's talk about shelter and protection comes into play. We will find genuine shelter when we rest in God, trusting our lives without expecting reward or gain. Nothing can separate us from God's love and care in that place. Our lives, with all their hurts and imperfections, are finally and fully reconciled with our Creator. There, we experience joy and peace beyond all understanding.

Under the majestic palms, there is a place of shade;
shelter from the onslaught of the sun's blistering rays.

Lest we lose heart, give up, and become afraid,
under the majestic palms, there is a place of shade.

When forces evil, unrelenting, and oppressive degrade,
we need God's enduring protection without delay.

Under the majestic palms, there is a place of shade;
shelter from the onslaught of the sun's blistering rays.

———————

There is an area around the base of a Palm tree called the root initiation zone. It is a place of constant growth as roots form, grow, and die. This specialized area is generally only about 40 inches, and the roots are not far below the soil. If a Palm stops producing new roots, it will die.

It makes me wonder about our need for mind, body, and spirit growth. What if we imagined growth not only at our extremities but at our roots? And what if we didn't just extend our current roots but formed new ones?

Let's return to the story of the Prodigal Sons. Notice I said, "sons." There are two. The first son ran away. When he returned, the Father welcomed him back into the household's shelter with grace and forgiveness. The second son finds himself outside the shelter of grace because he refuses to reconcile with his brother. You could say that he refuses to grow new roots in the soil of compassion and gratitude.

We return to the thoughts of a servant in that household. Might this have been on their mind?

And so we put on the biggest celebration the estate has ever known.

Reflecting on the days following the prodigal son's return, I see now how joy-filled those days were. With the wayward son home, the master's broken heart was mended, and the household delighted in the
master's excitement.

All was good. Well, it was somewhat good.

There was a big problem with the older son. He did not share his father's enthusiasm.

At first, it was an unspoken resentment. He wasn't happy with the over-the-top reception his father had given his undeserving brother. It escalated. The elder brother refused to come to the feast; worse, he refused to speak to his younger sibling.

Even after the master spoke to his first son, the son wouldn't yield. Self-righteous indignation prevented him from showing a shred of mercy.

My spirit is heavy once again for my master. As one son returns, he seems to have lost the other son. Instead of running away to a foreign land of forbidden pleasures, the older son has retreated inward to a dark place of hatred and judgment absent of all pleasure. And my master's heart breaks again.

I despairingly watch the drama, knowing I can't fix or repair this breach.

In the shadows of a cloudy night, I wait with sorrow for my master. I pray that time will heal and the older son will come to his senses. I yearn for another prodigal to return and enter joy's shelter.

This fictional story comes as a composite creation from the experiences of various folks.

With her cane by her side, Abigail sits in a rocking chair on the balcony of her high-rise condominium. A large palm tree partially obstructs her western view of the Gulf. Regularly, this perch provides spectacular sunset views. Abby enjoys them all.

Rocking back and forth, she reminisces about the journey to this place.

Abby didn't grow up in Florida and never wanted to leave Wisconsin. She always liked the cold and snow, especially since she didn't have to shovel it— her kids always took care of that. When job promotions moved them south, Abby agreed to follow them to the land of oranges and swaying palm trees.

Her family continues to bring her the greatest joy, and she is thankful to have a place near her kids and grandkids. However, many of her new friends aren't so lucky. Many live thousands of miles away from their families and have to arrange airfare to have dinner with their offspring.

Those circumstances differ from what Abby knew growing up on her parent's farm in Wisconsin.

Back then, it was a tight community where generations of the same family lived on the same parcels of land. Everyone knew everyone's business. There were troubles, and sometimes the drama was a bit much. Still, folks cared and watched out for each other. When someone ran into hard times, others stepped up.

Abby chuckled. Now, when one of her neighbors went to the hospital, she couldn't find out what happened. Sometimes, it would take the rumor mill weeks before folks discovered a death occurred.

Families didn't always share that information. Even the church wouldn't know until months later that long-time members died. Funerals often happened "up north" with no local chance to say goodbye.

The sense of community "down here" was different. It was constantly forming, with folks moving in and out. You had to be proactive about meeting friends; otherwise, you would be alone.

Whereas it is hard to argue with the beautiful sunshine weather, this "retired paradise" had its challenges. Distance from families and the transiency of neighbors were only two of them.

Affordable housing and unrestricted development strained the overall community's well-being. Abby thought about her cleaning lady. Daniela has three small children and lives forty-five minutes away.

Each morning, she leaves the house around five and joins the traffic heading into Naples. Her children need to get themselves together and are brought to school by a neighbor. Although Daniela is married, she rarely sees her husband, whose work regularly takes him out of state. They work long hours to put food on the table and gas in the aging vehicles.

Daniela is a good worker, even if she has difficulty speaking English. Abby, a retired English teacher, often thinks about providing language lessons. But Daniela always seems busy; there were always more houses to clean. With her long commute and high expenses, she didn't have the luxury to stop.

Luxury. It bothered Abigail that multi-million dollar homes with equally expensive yachts moored in the backyard were vacant for most of the year. Think of all the good that excess wealth could do. There was such disparity between those who had too much and those who struggled for so little.

But what was one to do?

Abigail often struggled with that question. Her social-minded conscience kept her engaged with local organizations that tried to balance the scales of biblical justice. Abby was sure that the prophet Amos would have had a field day with the mansions and yachts that got used a few weeks out of the year. Instead of "fat cows," she wondered if Amos might have used the image of "fat manatees" if he was in Florida. More chuckles.

On a more serious note, Abby was discouraged that her strained health prevented her from volunteering as she once did. Years ago, she was a regular at her church's soup kitchen and participated in all the community food collections. People needed food and dignity, and safety nets needed tending and mending. These passions continued to flame within her even if she couldn't do what she once did.

So as she slowed the rhythm of her rocking to view the sun better as it slipped behind the horizon, she prayed for inspiration, inspiration that might lead to a slice of paradise for Daniela and her community, just as she and her community enjoyed.

———————

One of the joys of living in this place called "paradise" is that you get visitors. The pages of our guest book are rapidly filling with friends, former neighbors, parishioners from previous parishes, and family. Some come for a day or overnight, while others stay the week. Our guest bedroom in Minnesota was never as busy as in Bonita Springs.

My wife Katie and I enjoy extending hospitality. Come one, come all. We love to reconnect and share our new tropical home. It is fun to take folks around to see the sights, dine at some of our favorite restaurants, and share sunsets.

With guidebooks on wildlife and fauna, we look up answers to all sorts of questions. As a result, we can identify at least a dozen different shells, half as many palms, and scads of birds. Although we are not yet informed enough to drive the tourist trolley, we increase our knowledge base with each visit. We do okay.

Visitors bring excitement. Days of preparation and planning precede festivities. Texts and phone calls escalate, anticipating the arrival. Shopping trips stock the refrigerator and bar. Our usually clean home gets a double go-over and scrub. The tiles and hard surfaces shine.

We count the days before our guests show up, cherish our moments with them, and catch our breath when they depart. The cycle repeats. Our laundry room wall calendar keeps the schedule. There are lots of names and lots of smiles. We are grateful to have such wonderful folks who want to spend time with us. Paradise's sunshine doesn't turn anyone away.

This chapter has focused on shelter. Even in the midst of great struggles and trials, we can rest and trust in Jesus's love, which finds great expression on the tree of the cross. This shelter of enduring love not only comforts us but it challenges us to go and do likewise. Share with love and shelter others in need.

At times, "sheltering in love" is easier said than done. Life can be messy and complicated. We get distracted, sidetracked, and overwhelmed. There is so much to do that it is easy to forget or overlook the needs of others. But even where there is focus and realization, another challenge presents as a barrier to action.

We may not like or understand the other person. Their way of life may not be our own, and we may find little in common with them. They are strangers, neither family nor friends. Worse yet, feelings of hatred might fester within us. They might have done us wrong or be the scapegoats for all that is wrong in our lives. What do we do with our enemies?

Jesus was clear on this matter: Love 'um. But how is that possible in a real and tangible way? How can we move from theory to practice?

Those palm trees we have been considering this week might provide a little help—in a word, flexibility. When hurricane winds generate adverse conditions, palm trees bend. Instead of rigidly resisting, palm trees give and go with the flow. Leaves might break off, but the main trunk rides out the storm.

What would it look like if we did the same? How might flexibility of heart, mind, and spirit allow us to connect with enemies, strangers, and even downright stinkers? Grounded in Jesus' love, what would it look like to bend in love with kindness, compassion, and generosity?

Reconciliation begins when we are willing to let go of the perceived and genuine hurts of the past so that we might have a different future with another. Again, this isn't easy, but it is essential to breaking estrangement's cycle. Instead of winning, we need to be willing to lose so that we might reconnect and establish a better relationship going forward.

Here, we can take direction from another tree— Jesus's cross. When Jesus discussed taking up the cross and following him, I wonder if he wasn't discussing reconciliation's difficult and essential work. As Christ reconciled God to us all through the selfless, sacrificial act of giving his life in love, forgiving even those who nailed him to the cross, following Jesus invites us to make courageous sacrifices.

What about self-abnegation and our worth? How do we honor the person God created us to be in the face of those who have continued to harm us and dehumanize us? Doesn't giving in and losing allow bad and destructive behavior to escalate unchecked?

Reconciliation is never easy and should not come at the expense of our created personhood. Abuse and violence are not acceptable outcomes and must be stopped. "Making peace" should not be confused with enabling or perpetuating destructive behavior.

That said, in our culture, there is an unhealthy inflation of the ego. Remembering that the universe does not revolve around us would do us well. Our wants are not more important than the needs of others. Our worth depends upon the value we share with everyone else - we are created in the image of God. We are not worth any more or any less than anyone else. Embracing our God-given value places us on equal footing with others, not above them. Humility grounds us in love and allows us to find common ground with all sorts of neighbors.

Sheltered in the shade of God's love, let us humbly embrace the challenge of reconciliation. With a spirit of openness, let us sway and be flexible, allowing Christ's love to work something new and wonderful inside us as new relationships form outside us. Who knows what joy we will encounter as enemies become acquaintances, strangers become friends, and we prepare our homes to welcome all, even unknown guests.

CHAPTER SIX: SUNSETS

"As they came near the village to which they were going, he walked ahead as if he were going on. But they urged him strongly, saying, "Stay with us, because it is almost evening and the day is now nearly over." So he went in to stay with them. When he was at the table with them, he took bread, blessed and broke it, and gave it to them. Then their eyes were opened, and they recognized him; and he vanished from their sight."

Luke 24: 28-31

One of my favorite things to do on a Sunday evening is to take a beach chair and catch a sunset. I have found it to be a restorative practice that does not disappoint. Sitting and watching the setting sun inch across the sky toward the horizon, peacefulness emerges. Matching deep breaths to the rhythmic sound of the waves, I settle into the calm serenity of it all.

The coasts of the Floridian peninsula are ideal for watching the daily rise and fall of our planet's sun: sunrise on the east coast and sunset on the west coast. Both are spectacular in their own right. No matter the photographer's skill, even the best pictures miss something of the experience. Sunsets and sunrises are something to behold.

Symbolically, sunrise and sunset can be conceived as beginnings and ends of days and chapters in life. There is movement into day and night. Feelings of hope, joy, and anticipation mix with completion, sadness, and regret. Perhaps a sense of melancholy tugs at our hearts as daytime runs out and night begins. We become simultaneously aware of the preciousness of each day and the paradox of time. Though time seems endless, our days are numbered. Each day completed is one less that we get to live.

Less we slip into depressing despair; faithful gratitude reminds us to praise God, the Creator of life and maker of the celestial bodies that move in the heavens. Though we are on temporal journeys, the Eternal One accompanies our travels through celestial cycles and seasons.

Sunsets anticipate sunrises. Dusk welcomes dawn. Night awaits day.

Awareness of such things brings needed balance and perspective in an otherwise frantic and disconnected culture obsessed with short-term gains and satisfactions. In our fast-paced digital world, there is motivation to bounce from one thing to the next with increased speed. There is a rush to hyperactivity that craves more. At times, we might feel overwhelmed trying to keep current on all the latest and greatest. In the flurry of it all, our spirits fall exhausted or become stressed to breaking points.

Instead of a natural rhythm attuned to the sun's cycles of rise and fall, day and night, we might find ourselves stuck in the unnatural state of perpetual noon. Instead of waking, engaging, and resting - we run constantly at the unhealthy speed of full steam. Breaking down is inevitable.

But there is another way. The biblical notion of the Sabbath offers a healthier path for us to travel, one attuned to natural cycles of night and day, sunset and sunrise. As we set aside time for rest and worship, we enter a pattern of stopping and starting, of slowing down, of awareness and intentions.

God created us to be part of a larger movement of suns and stars, placing us in a complex network of relationships. We are part of a creation that cycles between day and night, sunrise and sunset, and seasons of life and death. The Sabbath notices such things and delights in and celebrates them.

Observing such movements will positively impact our seeking and finding God. By breathing deeply, embracing morning and evening as unique opportunities for rising and resting, and considering our place in relation to the rest of creation, we will edge closer to our Creator. Or at least, we will gain a heightened awareness of the God who is already as close as the next breath of air that we take into our being that brings life and animates our existence. Joy ensues from such pursuits.

We begin the final chapter of this book with the guiding images of sunsets.

So grab your metaphorical beach chair and find a good spot on the beach. Settle into the chair and stretch your legs out on the sand. Take a deep breath as you gaze out onto the horizon. Notice the sky with its blending colors of yellow and orange.

Reflect upon the day that comes to a close. What were its ups and downs, triumphs and failures? Honor the varied relationships in which you shared in love's dance. Seek pardon where you mis stepped and missed connecting. Celebrate those moments where you caught glimpses of God's presence.

Smile and enjoy the beauty of a sunset, the close of another day. Welcome night as it emerges around you. Trust in God's care as you close your eyes to rest. Breathe.

––––––––

I've lost track of the number of sunsets I've seen since moving to Florida. This is not bragging; it is just to say that sunset watching has become a regular part of my life here on the Gulf Shore.

My wife Katie and I often head to the beach for a sunset walk along the surf. It is always relaxing and different. On some nights, we see a fiery orb descend into the watery horizon; on other nights, clouds obscure the sun's setting entirely. There are usually beautiful colors that dazzle, sometimes spectacularly so.

With every sunset, no matter how magnificent, there is always the end of daylight. We usually leave in the rapidly darkening twilight. By the time we arrive at the short-distance home, it is dark.

Sunsets mark the end of the daytime. Metaphorically, sunsets can symbolize the end of significant chapters in our lives or the conclusion of our lives themselves.

After Jesus's triumphant entrance into Jerusalem, the sun was setting on his public ministry. Events escalated, bringing about his arrest, trial, conviction, and crucifixion. In the Synoptic Gospels (Matthew, Mark, and Luke), Jesus's "cleansing" actions in the Temple seem to push the religious establishment over the edge in their desire to execute him. The Gospel of John is different.

Before Jesus's resurrection, the Gospel of John records the resurrection of a man named Lazarus by Jesus. According to the Fourth Gospel, this event was the proverbial straw that broke the camel's back of the religious establishment. Once Jesus demonstrated power over death, the head honchos in Jerusalem determined that he must be stopped at all costs. They felt threatened and took the political steps necessary that led to Jesus's crucifixion by the Roman authorities. Lazarus's resurrection was the turning point that hastened the sunset of Jesus's earthly ministry.

Let's imagine what Lazarus might have thought in the days following his resurrection. Might it have been something like this?

My name is Lazarus, and I should be dead. After all, my body was not able to fight the dreadful illness, and my breathing stopped. It was the sunset on my existence. Eleven days ago, I died.

For the last week, I have been trying to piece together what happened after that moment I slipped into nothingness.

My sister Martha, ever busy and working, told me about what the family did to grieve my passing. They wrapped my lifeless body in linen cloths and spices according to traditional burial practices. They put me in the family tomb and sealed that place which knows no sound.

Gone, I could not hear their wails of grief or see the tears that flowed from their eyes. Martha assured me she was distraught, and our sister Mary was inconsolable. Each sister did their best to cope and grieve in a manner consistent with their lifestyle. Mary pondered and sobbed in silence away from others while Martha kept busy, not allowing herself the time for tears.

Compounding their pain was the initial response that they received from our mutual friend, Jesus. Both Mary and Martha knew the stories told about him. Jesus was a healer. Not only were his words graceful and comforting, but he could cure miraculously. The blind received their sight. The lame walked. Those out of their minds, possessed by the very legions of Satan, received peace and cure. My sisters knew that as bad and threatening as my illness was, it did not compare with these other conditions. Surely, Jesus could heal their brother.

What is more, it was no secret. Jesus befriended us a while ago. Whenever his travels brought him near, he was a guest at our table. We would talk together long into the night, laughing and relaxing in each other's easy company. What friend wouldn't drop everything and help out?

When Martha sent word to Jesus, it was with urgency: " Come quickly, your friend Lazarus is fading." I'm surprised she didn't go herself, but she wouldn't abandon my care for a minute. Mary held my hand and stayed close by. Martha was in and out with fresh water and clean cloth. I was never alone.

If effort and love alone could cure, I would have instantly recovered. But that isn't how life or illness work. There are times when no matter how hard you try and no matter what medicines you use, death still comes as an uninvited intruder. Our prayers don't always turn out as we'd like them to. And so it was.

It took Jesus four days to arrive. By then, I was not only sealed tight in the tomb, but my body was showing signs of decay. The mourning ritual was in full swing with family and friends gathered. I'm sure Mary and Martha weren't the only ones disappointed with Jesus's tardiness. No doubt there was a cold stare or two in that bunch. Silent disapproval and the shaking of a head greeted the traveling preacher.

As folks described the situation to me, I'm surprised anyone let Jesus near the tomb. It was one thing to heal, but what chance do miracles have after four days? Again, I was dead and decaying. There was no chance of resuscitation.

Was it the curious words Jesus spoke to my sister that gained him access to the burial cave? He told Martha, "I am the resurrection and the life." Or maybe it was the tears he cried with Mary that allowed him to proceed. Perhaps their inexplicable and combined faith paved the way for what followed.

"Lazarus, come out!"

To be continued...

———————

The following fictional story is inspired by observations during the annual collegial bacchanal festivities known nationally as "Spring Break."

The three friends giggled as they pushed each other playfully on the sand. Suzanne, Jeni, and Christine had "survived" the drama and frivolity of a Spring Break together. Overall, it was a good week full of sun and fun. They went to the beach daily to lie in the sun, read, and chill. They enjoyed themselves while avoiding too much sunburn.

It was the last night of their week-long vacation, and they decided to go to the beach for one last sunset. After stacking their coverups and jean shorts in a pile, they scampered into the gentle surf, wearing swimsuits of varying modesty. Each held their cell phone, ready for a series of ensuing selfies.

These weren't the first pictures and wouldn't be the last of their adventure a thousand miles from their Midwest University. Throughout their college years, thousands of images captured in pixels the journey of learning and discovery that brought them closer to unraveling their essential identities. Spring Break was the latest chapter in the exponentially expanding book of their lives.

Suzanne, Jeni, and Christine were about as different as they come. Suzanne was a Minnesota farm girl, Jeni was from New York City, and Christine was from Birmingham, Alabama. None of their majors aligned: Chemistry, Political Science, and Art History. Christine was ready to graduate in May, while Jeni and Suzanne still had too many credits to complete to consider graduation.

Somehow, fate conspired to bring them together as "besties." Two years ago, random housing assignments put them in the same dorm. Friendship flowed easily, and they decided to share off-campus housing. From that point onward, they were inseparable.

Silhouetted against the amber sky, they smiled and laughed at the handheld cameras on selfie mode. They were beautiful against nature's artistic background, and the shots and videos were animated with a youthful zest. A carefree attitude permeated the ad-hoc photo shoot.

At that moment, they didn't have a care in the world. The future was on hold, yielding to the unscripted joy of the present. Even Christine, who was the planner and thinker of the group, forgot about schedules, grades, graduation, and job searches. Nothing detracted from the blissful experience they shared. Anxieties placed no strain. All three breathed a deep sigh, full of life.

Although that moment was digitally collected and stored for prosperity, it would live beyond megabytes as a time remembered in their hearts. Their lives were about to undergo significant changes. Christine's graduation would commence life beyond the walls of an institute of higher education. Suzanne and Jeni would need to find another housemate or return to the dorms. Would they stay in touch or fade apart?

Although none of them were in a serious romantic relationship, those would come and present more challenges to their friendship. Love, real and imagined, always needed expression and navigation. Heartaches and heartthrobs would all have their time going forward as they did in the past. With each, love teaches lessons that don't appear on a syllabus. Love's capacity grows even through difficulties and challenges.

As the sun disappeared into the expansive Gulf horizon, they were metaphorically and literally at the end of a day. Tomorrow, changes would come with the repeating cycles of night and morning. Travels needed to be taken as journeys continued down uncertain paths. Friendship and love would continue and look different. One last look at the camera. Smile.

———————

When looking at photos, it is often difficult to determine whether it is a picture of a sunset or a sunrise. Both celestial events involve a similar color palette of bright yellows, oranges, and reds that push against purple, indigo, and blue. Whenever the closest star in our galaxy, and therefore brightest in relation to us, nears the horizon, there is the potential for a spectacular showing. Radiation, atmosphere, and light rays blend, mix, and conflict in ways truly pleasing to the eyes, heart, and soul.

There is something special and sacred in the passage from day to night and vice versa. Here, time finds demarcation. One day is distinguished from another, allowing us to record and note its particularity. For thousands of years around the globe, humans have noticed and documented solar movements and the transition from one day to another as the sun rises and sets.

Although we might think of midnight as the official start of the day, in Jewish thought and tradition, the day begins and ends at sundown. Instead of sunrise, sunset marks a beginning. That is why all Jewish holidays and Sabbaths start at sundown. This tradition finds grounding in the first biblical creation account in Genesis; "And there was evening, and there was morning, the first day (Genesis 1:5)."

It is hard to imagine celebrating the New Year and welcoming the next year on the Gregorian calendar[8] at sunset. As a kid, I would have felt jilted not getting to stay up late, eat snacks, and make noise at midnight. The ball drop at Times Square in New York City, with all its New Year's festivities, wouldn't be the same if everyone was looking for the sun to kiss the horizon, which is not easily seen from midtown.

Suspending beloved traditions and the dominant calendar for a moment, there is some wisdom and perspective found in the time/day tradition Jesus knew as a Jew in the first century. Starting the day at sunset recognizes night before day, darkness before light.

It may seem counterintuitive to start a day at the moment the sun disappears beyond the horizon and nighttime descends. For most folks, night is time for rest, not when they go to work. Shouldn't we be productive as early as possible? Resting first doesn't sit well with my work ethic.

Besides, the night is a little scary. You can't see all that surrounds you and must be careful as you walk about. Tripping hazards abound. And then there are the dangers that lurk in the dark and go bump in the night. There is a good reason that horror movies excessively use shadows and dark places to generate terror—we are frightened by what we can't fully see.

---

[8] Note: The Gregorian calendar, established by Pope Gregory XIII in 1582, is the most used worldwide. It modified the earlier Julian calendar and gave us leap years.

So why would you ever start the day in the dark?

In a word, the biblical answer is "creation." At the start of creation, before even the whole concept of days and time began, before the suns and planets established orbits, there was darkness and chaos. In the primordial soup, before life as we know it took shape, form, and purpose, our Creator entered the void of nothingness and got to work. God pulled and tugged, brought matter and energy together, ordered light and voilà! The Creator birthed creation across eons of time and space beyond imagination.

Inspired by the Creator's work at the start of creation, starting the day in the dark isn't as bizarre as it might seem. Night is the canvas upon which God begins a masterpiece. In the darkness, God speaks a word of life, which brings light. Out of seemingly nothing, dark and dead, God works.

This brings us hope. When we find our lives lifeless or in chaos, the conditions are right for God to work something new and lively. Each sunset, twilight, and night anticipates sunrise, dawn, and a new day. At least this movement is consistent with the creative workings of our Creator, whose bias is life and love.

Beginning the day at sunset involves trusting God's protection, care, and presence while we take our nightly rest. It is time for a sacred pause as we go to sleep.

Magnificent colors blending across the sky,
while the sun's fleeting rays upon the water glisten.

Another day is over, gone by.
Magnificent colors blending across the sky.

Night descends; rest beckons us to lie
still upon our beds; for God we listen.

Magnificent colors blending across the sky,
while the sun's fleeting rays upon the water glisten.

The imaginative story continues of a resurrected Lazarus. What might he have felt like shortly after Jesus raised him from the dead? How did the experience of resurrection to new life play out in his story days before Jesus's crucifixion and resurrection?

Sadness washes over me when I think about the pain my sisters and friends endured on account of my death. Being resurrected means I have been fully restored to all of life. "All" means everything, including the heartache and suffering. What I put my poor family through replays as a nightmare.

Thankfully, I can also enjoy the freshness of a morning as the sun rises, breathing deeply of the sweetness. Each day brings an opportunity to enjoy living and generously share it with loved ones. Praise God from whom all blessings flow!

I have been given more than just another chance to live. My resurrection has given me a new perspective on life. I no longer take things for granted. Now that I know how fragile and fleeting it can be, I resolve not to waste a moment of this precious life.

Earlier this evening, Jesus came by the house for dinner. It was like old times to have our dear friend with us. Even Martha let the dirty dishes sit on the table to join the conversation. Joy filled each of us to the point that we were almost giddy. Mary laughed without restraint, and even Jesus got into it. What a pleasure to be together and to be alive.

Such feelings come at a good time of the year. Passover is in just six days. It is a shame that we won't be able to celebrate the ritual meal with Jesus, but he mentioned the importance of being alone with his disciples that day. Although they have been traveling with him for the better part of three years, there are always things a Teacher must teach their pupils.

Tomorrow, Jesus will enter Jerusalem. The village is abuzz with talk that the crowd will celebrate the entrance. How could they not? Word has spread after my resurrection in front of the entire village. They call Jesus the Messiah, the Chosen One of the Most High God. And I don't disagree. How could I? Only the One who comes in the name of the Lord has the power to resurrect. And there is no arguing that I was resurrected.

I wonder how Jesus's opponents will disagree now. The resurrection of the dead evokes a belief that is hard to refute. The religious establishment would be foolish to work against Jesus, given his popularity and power. Still, there is a danger if they feel threatened. Maybe Jesus shouldn't go into the Holy City.

I imagine the chief priests, scribes, and Pharisees would stop at nothing to preserve their slipping influence and power. I'm sure that they would even collaborate with those heathen Romans to bring a sunset to Jesus's ministry and following. Crosses loom on the horizon, I fear.

But to kill the Messiah? Would God allow such blasphemy? Such questions haunt me to the depth of my spirit.

My faith is an important part of my renewed convictions. When Jesus commanded my body to come out of the tomb, he also drove my spirit out of the darkness. Come out! Enter into the light and life of a new day.

Lose the trappings and bondage of the past. Forgive and be forgiven. Dwell in mercy, not judgment. Allow grace to open the most remote places of heart, mind, and intuition. Receive, honor, and celebrate God's presence within the self, others, and the connected spaces between.

Jesus gave me more than extended existence; he gave me a new life! I follow with gratitude the One who creates life, resurrects it and connects it with all living creatures. From the night following sunset comes the sunrise and a new day. Thanks be to God!

———————

Walking along the beach at sunset, I often find myself in a reflective mood. For some reason, introspection comes easily as the sky turns orange. Maybe because even a crowded beach will quiet itself down to watch nature's nightly celestial show.

For twenty-five years, I served as a pastor in traditional congregational settings. Faith Lutheran Church in New Providence, New Jersey, and St. James Lutheran Church in Burnsville, Minnesota, were suburban congregations. Generations of folks came to worship, and you had the privilege to watch children grow up and families age. Simultaneously, you ministered to every age group across two and sometimes three generations.

Things are a little different at Christus Victor Lutheran, Naples. It is a seasonal place where a large majority of folks are not relatives and have only been together for a short period of time. Only a few families in attendance have multi-generations. Most are retired or semi-retired and have moved into the area.

At Christus Victor Lutheran, lives are connected for a while. There are seasonal comings and goings. For some, the annual migration lasts from a couple of weeks to six months. For others, this might be the only year they rent in the area. Some of our most engaged participants have been "seasonal" for decades.

There is another aspect of seasonality that finds expression at Christus Victor Lutheran. A pattern exists where folks attend after moving into the area during the retirement or pre-retirement "season" of their lives. They might rent in the area for a little while, enjoy the warm sunshine and all the activities, and decide to move into more permanent living accommodations. Many of these "transplants" will spend a few decades in the area until life circumstances force a move. Some will move to senior living facilities locally. Others will move back "up north" to be closer to family.

Finally, I've observed a "season" in people's health. Often they move to the sunshine state in good health, yearning to do all the active things that perpetual sunshine allows: golf, pickleball, kayaking, boating, fishing, hiking, and so on. They will do all these things, enjoying the vitality that comes with them, until their health fails. Often they are well into the seventh or eighth decade of life before their health sours. When this happens it forces adjustments in lifestyle.

As a pastor in such a seasonal context, I experience joy and sorrow amid the comings and goings. As "the season" begins, it is wonderful to greet folks as they return. From October through March, Sunday morning attendance swells weekly. A pastoral colleague likens the energy during the season on a Sunday morning to that of Christmas Eve. Folks are happy to "be back." And I am grateful to have them back.

The pain comes with sunset. Even in the Sunshine State, endless summer days come to a close. There is a time of goodbyes, and these vary in duration. As seasons end, we part. For some, it is a "see you later" - they will return next October, January, or February. For others, it is more permanent; "We sold our place and won't be coming back."

Sunsets abound in seasonal communities and can be hard on the heart.

You might say that "paradise" isn't the only place people move to, where folks retire and health changes. And you are right. I've experienced all these things elsewhere. No matter where life is lived, it has a seasonal quality. As human creatures, we move through stages and seasons. With this movement comes patterns of joy and sorrow, welcome and farewell. We rejoice, and we grieve— sometimes simultaneously.

Good Friday teaches that with each sunset comes the promise of Easter sunrise. The cross of Christ, with all its anguish, is not the end of our relationship with Jesus. Though all might seem lost, changed, or moved as Calvary's Day draws to a close, there is still another chapter in our story with God.

Sunset - sunrise. God works at night to bring about something wonderfully new and life-generative. Easter morning is on its way. An empty tomb is right around the proverbial corner.

The story of God's love that Jesus preached, taught, and embodied in an open, inclusive table fellowship continues. Resurrection is on the way. Joy has another chance to unfold in an enhanced manner.

I find great hope in such God-realities. Though I tear up as the goings increase and grieve departures, they are a necessary part of our seasonal lives. I am grateful for the time we spend together and the wonderful relationships we are privileged to have. Whether folks are in our lives for a little while or many years, there is a blessing for us to celebrate.

God has brought us together, and our paths have crossed. Fortune permits us the opportunity to learn from and love one another. Because of our interaction, we are changed, and we will never be the same. More gratitude is due. Even when the experience wasn't the greatest, there is potential for a positive learning outcome.

I may not welcome saying "goodbye," and I prefer to keep things as they are. But, I haven't found the magical wand to wave and make it so. Such magic doesn't exist. There is nothing I can do to keep the sun from setting. However, this I can do: I can embrace sunset with joyful gratitude.

So let me wipe my eyes and say a heartfelt thanks. Thank you, God, for the day that comes to a close. Thank you, folks, for sharing these moments with me, adventures well taken. Thank you for the ups and downs, successes and failures, challenges and opportunities. Thank you for the love given and shared among us and beyond. Thank you for the memories, little and large. I am filled with joy as I wait for sunrise.

CONCLUSION

Southwest Florida is not paradise, nor is Hawaii or any of the numerous Caribbean or South Pacific islands. Sure, there are waves, sand, exotic birds, palm trees, and sunsets against the backdrop of an endless summer with abundant sunshine. In these places, there is relaxation, renewal, and retirement aplenty. Still, paradise eludes.

A true paradise, that place of perfection and harmony, where all are content, connected, and at peace, remains unattainable on this side of mythic Eden. At best, we catch but glimpses of that place God imagined and intended for humanity to dwell.

Perhaps we should think of "paradise" as a state of mind or being instead of a place. Inspired by God's dream of a community where all have dignity and worth, all relationships are grounded in love and mercy, and all creation is stewarded with the utmost care and respect.

It sounds impossible—perhaps—but it was a dream that inspired the life, death, and resurrection of Jesus, who was from the village of Nazareth, far from the places of power and prestige in the ancient

Roman world. Glimpses of paradise were found in the healing, teaching, and table fellowship of the one who is called Christ, or God's Chosen One. Including those excluded by the holy and self-righteous establishment of the time, Jesus engaged everyone from poor to wealthy, all genders, and even those judged to be sinful and enemies.

Joy was a byproduct of Jesus's embodiment of God's dream of a redeemed Eden. If but for a moment, joy lived in the most unlikely places and among those unaccustomed to the happiness afforded in this life. In the final moments of his earthly life, Jesus extended paradise to a criminal on a nearby cross; "Today, you will be with me in paradise (Luke 23:43)."

Wrapped in God's promise and presence, paradise is a gift from a gracious and loving God. Despite the assertions and proclamations of cultures supercharged with commercialism and self-interest, it can't be bought or manufactured. Instead, it must be sought, discovered, cherished, and shared.

This book began with a quote from St. Augustine about our endless search for that paradise connection with God: "Thou hast made us Thyself, and our hearts are restless till they rest in Thee."

As the sun shines through the stained-glass window from the closed church of my childhood, casting light colors upon the floor of my church study, I am reminded daily of Augustine's words inscribed on the window. They offer welcomed wisdom to this spiritual traveler: There will always be restlessness in every earthly and manufactured paradise.

No matter how gentle and warm the surf, how soft and playful the sand, how exotic and beautiful the birds, how rare and exquisite the shells, how majestic and tall the palms, or how magnificent and memorable the sunset - there will always be something missing in life as long as we are apart from our Creator.

Whether our hearts are on vacation or hard at work, as they pursue joy and pleasure away from God and God's way of life, there will be frustration. Something will be missed. Our balance and peace will be off. Only when we turn towards God (the biblical notion of repentance) do we begin to find rest for our souls.

This is not to say that we can arrive at such a place this side of eternal paradise. We cannot, at least not fully. There will always be some part of our heart, mind, or body that remains a bit restless.

That said, thankfully, we will catch a glimpse from time to time. Through intentionality, prayer, worship, love, care of others, and mindfulness, we open ourselves and become more aware of God's nearness. With awareness comes peace and joy.

Whether we do or do not move in this intentional direction, by the grace of God, God's Spirit is constantly moving in and among us, inviting and prodding us in love. Love is, after all, the language and essence of God, and it is always in motion flowing in and out of the many relationships in which we find ourselves.

Breathing attunes our heart, mind, and spirit with an awareness that brings rest. Even in the most crowded spaces or stressful situations, we can find respite as we breathe deeply. Recently, in a conversation with friends who also practice mindful/contemplative breathing, I shared my gratitude for these practices whenever I have to wait in an ER or endure a medical test patiently. Breathing lowers my anxiety and blood pressure gifting calmness amid calamity. I am grateful whenever I am in a stressful situation that I have already practiced intentional breathing.

Seeking rest in God through breathing is one way of pursuing our hearts' lifelong quest. As mentioned, other forms of prayer, worship, compassion, kindness, and positive interactions with others and creation are all part of constantly seeking God.

They also help train our senses to recognize God, who is always near. When intentional about our faith lives, we are more apt to 'find' God. This is not because God is hiding from us, although there is an aspect of God that will always be mysterious. God doesn't hide, but so much gets in our way of perceiving. Many barriers make it hard for us to grasp a presence so near.

A lot of these barriers are internal. There is "stuff" inside us all that will block the flow of God's Spirit through us. Love, mercy, and grace get hung up by past experiences, our cultural engagement, biases, knowledge, and our emotions. Even our belief system and deeply held convictions can get in the way if they lack the inclusive and radical nature of Christ's love. Recall, the Pharisees were extremely religious and practiced beloved traditions while opposing and blocking Jesus's life and ministry.

When we block God's love from flowing through us, we are likely to experience a lack of joy in our restlessness. We might find that anger festers within us. Combined with fear, this is a dangerous combination that has led others to places of unspeakable violence. We must be careful.

This leads back to our need to seek God. Searching for God's presence each day is not only good for our souls but also desperately needed in our world. In divisive times when people are bitter, hurting, isolated, and lonely, it is more important than ever for people of faith to seek our loving God.

Searching high and low, like the woman who lost her coin or the shepherd his sheep, requires persistent effort. Consider also the father whose prodigal sons have wandered away from his love; he waited, looking at the horizon and outside the feast hall, for his sons to come to their senses. All these characters in Jesus's parables were not disappointed. For they found that which their hearts desired and it brought immeasurable joy. They had to celebrate.

And so it is with all journeys that seek God. There is the promise of finding, joy, and celebration. Even if it is only a glimpse, we shall see God's presence along our spiritual quest.

I conclude this devotional full of joy, with the sure and certain hope of God's paradise. With Easter on my heart and spirit, I smile from the inside out. May joy find its way to where you find yourself today as you seek and find God. May images from and blessings of paradise increase your faith until that day when we will rest securely forever in God's paradise.

QUESTIONS TO PONDER

Chapter One: Waves

How do waves affect you? What experiences do you have with waves?

In what ways might waves inspire you?

Have you ever been in a bad storm? How did that feel? How did you survive?

Where was God in the midst of your storm?

Can you think of a time when you had to adjust your plans because of something beyond your control? How did you deal with the situation? What resources did you use? Where was God?

What is your vocation? Where does your joy (skills, talents, etc) meet a great need? How might you lean into what God has given to help out?

When was the last time that you consciously breathed? Can you take a breath now?

What effect does closing your eyes and taking a deep breath have on your body? Mind? Spirit?

Can you think of a time when you were caught in a threatening storm? How did you hold on for life? What was it like when the storm finally ceased?

How do you rest in the peace of God?

How might your relationship with God be understood through the lens of parent and child?

What role does freedom and control play in your relationship with God? With others?

How might you focus today on your relationship with God?

How might focusing on your baptismal identity as a child of God provide direction and intention in your living?

Chapter Two: Sand

How do you follow in the footsteps of Jesus?
Which of your regular behaviors best imitate Jesus?
What is your reaction to the fictitious character Asher
and his judgments of the crowd that came to hear
Jesus?
On what basis do you judge others? In a crowd? On the
road? How quick do your judgments of others come?
Which of Jesus's teachings do you find the hardest to
follow?
Have you ever suffered a loss due to a natural disaster
or storm? What did you learn from that experience? How
has that experience shaped you?
Have you ever responded to calls for help and assistance
following a tragedy? Why? What did you learn from your
participation?
Where do you find God during challenging times?
What does it mean to you to have Jesus as a friend?
How does friendship with Jesus affect your other
friendships?
When did you change your mind last? What
circumstances brought about that change?
What changes might Jesus's love be seeking in you?
Where have you seen followers of Jesus come together in
service?
What are your experiences of helping those in need?
How is God present when folks gather to serve?
How does following Jesus bring comfort?
Where does following Jesus unsettle you and make you
restless?
How does the teaching of Jesus cling to you and seek to
shape you?

Chapter Three: Shorebirds

What does being a part of a "flock" mean?

How large is your "flock"? Is there room for more? How would you react to growth?

Who do you consider part of God's "flock"?

Have you ever felt abandoned or left out by your friend group or family? Can you think of a time when you excluded others?

What opportunities got missed? What challenges resulted?

How might God be calling you to be a good Samaritan to those who differ from you?

How do you respond to those who have different views? Do you react the same way in person as you do through social media outlets? If you respond differently, why do you think that is?

Have you had political differences cause a rift among your friends or family? What would it take to heal this division?

What might you be able to do today to show care to someone different from you?

How do you pursue biblical justice in your thoughts, words, and deeds?

What gets in the way of being part of God's dream for all?

Who is the least likely person to become your friend? How might the love of Jesus enable you to extend love to unlikely folks?

What volunteer experiences do you have? How did it feel to help out?

What opportunities do you have to volunteer your time and talents? How might you make time to give some time for a worthy cause?

Where might God be found in your volunteering?

How might the birds inspire you?

What lessons about flocking together might we glean from our feathered friends?

Where is God to be found in diversity?

Chapter Four: Shells & Driftwood

When have you been lonely or separated from others?
How has sin isolated you?
Where do you most need God's forgiveness, renewal, and refreshment?
Think of a time when you lost something valuable. How did you feel? Did you ever recover it?
Where is God amid our losing, searching, and finding?
Where is God as we grieve loss?
Have you ever experienced the joy that comes with finding something that you considered lost forever?
What impact does the experience of finding have on our spirits?
Where do you need God's forgiveness and grace?
How might God's love transform you today?
Have you ever forgotten something important that has led to a moment of despair or anxiety? Were you concerns relieved as you recalled?
What treasures, literal and metaphorical, have you lost?
Where might they be found?
Where is God in our seeking and finding?
Have you ever had an unexpected invitation at just the right time?
How might God be working through our and others invitations?
What is the difference between being by yourself and being lonely?
What reconnects you with others?
Where do we see God at work in our network of relationships?

Chapter Six: Sunsets

What are your experiences with sunrise/sunset? Have you seen any good ones recently?

What are the healthy patterns in your life? What about the unhealthy ones?

Where is God found in your daily routines of rising and resting?

Why do you think that Lazarus's resurrection was so threatening to the religious establishment?

What about Jesus's miracles or teachings do we find problematic?

Where does our faith need resurrecting?

Can you think of a time in your life when things were rapidly changing and things were both coming to an end and beginning all at once?

How did you feel during that time of transition?

Where was God present for you?

How might you in your nightly prayers recognize God's creative work in your life as you stop working and give your body the time to restore?

How might you welcome as night descends the possibility of a new day, gifted and crafted by our loving and gracious God?

What creative opportunities lie in the dark? How might God be at work while you rest?

How does Jesus bring you new life?

Where are you still in need of resurrection?

What gratitude might you express to God?

What season of life do you find yourself in?

Where is God present your season?

How do you express gratitude in your life?

Where have you caught glimpses of paradise? Of God?

What practices have you found helpful in your search for God's presence in your life?

How might you allow God's love to flow through you?

PRAYERS

Gracious and Loving God,
you swept over the waters
pushing chaos back.

When the rains come down,
and the waves batter my boat,
be present with me.

Give me new courage
and strengthen my weary soul;
allow faith to grow.

Amen.

Gracious and Loving God,
your Spirit moves over the waters,
bringing life and hope.

Move over the waves of my life,
and bring me to life - again.

Let your love swell in my heart,
that it overflows.
Flow through me
that my words and deeds
might bear your love in mercy
to others.

Through Christ,
who commanded the waves
to be still.

Amen.

Gracious Loving God,
our best-laid plans fall apart;
we find ourselves stuck.

Give needed wisdom,
that we might apply your gifts.
engage head, heart, hands.

Let us find our joy,
in compassionate service,
meeting the world's need.

Amen.

Source of all Living,
let me breathe deeply of you.
I breathe waves of joy.

Amen

O Bringer of Peace,
your voice calms rambunctious waves.
Settle my spirit down.
Allow me to breathe;
Help me to center in love.
Guide me to trust you.

Then from a still place,
transform praise into action.
From peace move to love.

Amen.

Gracious Loving God,
you offer your hand to guide,
showing me the way.

Yet, you do not force.
You give me freedom to run.
Foolishness prevails.

I chase distractions.
I break down, stumble, get lost.
I wander away.

Yet, your love finds me.
You extend your loving hand.
Mercy embraces.

Amen.

Gracious Loving God,
your love remains part of me.
You've claimed me - your own.

In you there is love,
throughout all the days of life,
In you there is joy.

Your blessings abound.
In awe, I extol your name!
Thanks and praise to you!

Amen.

Gracious Loving God,
you invite me to follow
in the way of Christ.

Allow Christ's values
to guide my living each day.
Strengthen me in grace.

Amen.

Gracious God,
through the words and actions of Jesus,
you teach us your way of life.

Sometimes, these lessons are hard,
challenging our assumptions,
perceptions, culture,
traditions, and convictions.

When we find your words abrasive,
give us the courage to continue listening.
Allow your word to transform
even the hardest places of our hearts.
Mold us to your loving ways
so that our lives align with yours.
Strengthen our faith
so we might better follow Jesus.

Amen.

Gracious Loving God,
in the midst of disaster,
and life falls apart,

we might all wonder -
why has God abandoned us?
Where did you go, God?

Our spirits might sag
as we ask troubled questions;
Our faith can falter.

Love allows questions;
God's steadfast love bears our pain
accompanying us.

Mysterious Friend,
even when we cannot see,
you are always near.

In shadows, sunshine,
blessings continue to flow,
from your gracious hand.

Amen.

Gracious Loving God,
what a friend we have in you!
You are always near.

Thank you for loving.
Thank you for sharing your care.
Thank you for being.

Allow our friendship
to mold and shape me in love.
Let love flow through me.

Amen.

Gracious Loving God,
provider of life and grace.
Shape me with your love.

Amen.

Gracious Loving God,
opportunity exists
where there is great need.

In destruction's wake,
compassion has work to do;
opened hearts engage.

Christ calls us to serve,
to become God's hands and feet
activating love.

And when we respond,
God will not leave us alone.
We will see Christ's face.

Amen.

Come, Lord Jesus, come!
Come, enter this heart of mine.
Change me in your love.

Shape me through your word.
Transform me in compassion.
Comfort in struggle.

Leave me not alone.
Through your life, guide all my ways.
Let me rest in you.

Amen.

Creator of all,
enlarge my vision to see,
your image in all.

Open my closed heart
to make space for those left out.
Expand my loving.

Amen.

God of my neighbors,
your love is for all people.
No one is beyond.

Expand my loving.
Increase imagination.
Let me know others.

Amen.

O Lover of all,
during times of division,
bring us together.

Heal our hurting hearts.
In the name of Jesus Christ,
give us common ground.

Allow Jesus love
to repair all brokenness;
make us whole again.

Amen.

Creator of all,
shape and mold me in your love.
Make me follow You.

Guide me in your ways;
let the life of Jesus teach
where to go now.

Form my life into
an instrument of your grace.
Flow freely through me.

Amen.

Creator Lover,
I let things get in the way
of loving like you.

I can close my heart;
on those who are strange to me.
I hold them away.

Give me the courage
that it takes to build bridges
and love's connections.

Jesus calm my fears
open my closed eyes to see
your face in neighbor.

Amen.

God with a full heart,
thank you for those who donate
time, talent, treasure.

Bless those who make time
and share with generous hearts.
In them we see You.

God, create in me
a spirit that gives away
and helps others out.

Amen.

Great and Holy One,
you created everyone.
Your image in all.

Give me the wisdom
to see your face in others.
Open my heart wide.

Help me to embrace
the complex diversity
of all you have made.

Let me be joyful
in constant celebration;
Praise be to you, God!

Amen.

Forgiving Jesus,
refresh us as we linger
in sinful dryness.

Let us find anew
a life connected with you,
and linked with others.

Forgiven, renewed
freely flow your love through us
delighting in joy.

Amen.

Abiding Jesus,
although you are always near,
sometimes I lose stuff.

I feel lost, lonely.
Grief can overwhelm my joy.
I plod solo, sad.

Though all might seem gone.
Remind me when I forget
that you are nearby.

Restore my lost joy.
Revive my celebration.
Your love has found me!

Amen.

God of all the lost,
be present to those who grieve,
let them find new peace.

Amen.

Gracious Forgiver,
Your love can reconnect us,
bridge the gap between.

Repair the broken
parts of our disjointed lives;
make us whole again.

Let love redirect
our energy and focus
to those beyond us.

Amen.

Gracious Living God,
Your love remains at all times,
Ev'n though I forget.

In all the busy,
in my frantic scurrying,
I get lost easily.

But, you don't get lost.
Your love is constant, endures.
Nothing can stop it.

Give me the wisdom,
that I might perceive you near.
Help me remember.
That I am beloved.
No matter what, I am yours.
Your compassion reins.

Amen.

O God, you invite
into your love and grace
and transform all life.

Be present today,
bring clarity to me now,
that I might perceive.

Let love guide vision.
Through loving acts of my own,
help me to respond.

Amen.

Gracious Loving God,
your love seeks to reunite
our fragmented lives.

In you there is hope
of resurrection, new life;
light shines in darkness!

Amen.

Comforting Shelter,
in your love there is always
a place for resting

In your cooling shade,
let me find relief today
from the sun's hot rays.

Refreshed and renewed
give me wisdom to repair
broken connections.

Let love flow through me
that I might be reconciled
from those I'm apart.

Amen.

Always forgiving,
God you meet me where I am;
with love you embrace.

In you, I find space.
In the shelter of your love,
a place for resting.

I raise thanksgiving
for your ongoing welcome
that brings me back home.

Amen.

Shelterer of All,
give me the wisdom needed,
to help my neighbor.

Allow love to guide
my thinking, words, and actions
so to follow you.

Amen.

Gracious Loving God,
throughout the struggles of life,
bring your gift of faith.

In your love's shelter;
let me find needed courage
to face all trials.

Let me rest in you;
at all times, even the bad.
Walk with me through night.

Then inspire me;
Guide my focus beyond me
shelter to provide.

Amen.

Gracious Loving God,
I don't always share your love.
I can be stingy.

I can be selfish.
Bruised feelings get in the way.
I have my reasons.

Transform me with grace.
Forgive me as I depart
from your ways of love.

Turn me inside out.
Foster generosity;
lead my heart onward.

Amen.

Creator of all,
from the place where I shelter,
give my heart vision.

Let me see the need,
of those whose shelter falters.
Inflame compassion.

Allow your great love
to excite passion within
to provide shelter.

Amen.

Loving Open Host,
your love reaches out to me,
inviting me in.

Give me the wisdom
to perceive and understand
the riches of grace.

Encourage within
a humble, willing spirit
to open my heart.

Inspire me now.
that I might provide shelter
to those who have need.

Amen.

Creator of Life,
bring to me an awareness
of you in each day.

Give me the courage
to rise at the start of day
with a full spirit.

Help me breathe deeply,
throughout the day's ups and downs.
Praising your presence.

Guide my trust in you,
when the day comes to a close.
Resting securely.

Amen.

Resurrected God,
you bring life where there is none;
Praise belongs to you!

God, please be present
in those places and those times
when life is strained - dead.

Call into the depths
of all dark and scary tombs-
"Lazarus, come out!"

Amen.

God of steadfast love,
when life goes through transitions
be present to me.

Calm all my worries;
Give me courage over fear.
Guide me in your ways.

Amen.

God of day and night,
your creating never stops
neither does your love.

When I go to sleep,
allow me to trust in you
and find my true rest.

Amen.

God who resurects,
bring life into those places
where death dwells within.

Create a new heart
where I have not loved others
resurrect my love.

Amen.

Gracious Loving God,
in all the seasons of life,
you are always near.

Bless as seasons change,
and in transitions we find
ourselves lingering.

Allow love to guide
to yourself and others
my wandering self.

Amen.

ONLINE RESOURCES

Online Devotional

You can access this book's content and *Inspirational Images* through daily email devotions at no additional cost.

To sign up, use this link:
http://www.lightfromthishill.com/full-of-joy-online-resources
When asked for a code, use the following (all caps): JOY

Online Faith Chats

Want to use this book in a small group setting? *Faith Chats* are designed for this purpose. You can download discussion sheets for each chapter from the Online Resources menu.

Use this link:
http://www.lightfromthishill.com/full-of-joy-online-resources
When asked for a code, use the following (all caps): JOY

ABOUT THE AUTHOR

The Rev. Dr. Walt Lichtenberger is an ordained pastor in the Evangelical Lutheran Church in America who has served three congregations: Faith Lutheran Church in New Providence, New Jersey, St. James Lutheran Church in Burnsville, Minnesota, and Christus Victor Lutheran Church in Naples, Florida.

In addition to over twenty-five years of parish experience, he holds three advanced theological degrees. In 1997, he graduated from the Lutheran Theological Seminary in Gettysburg, Pennsylvania, with a Master of Divinity. This was followed in 2006 with a Master of Sacred Theology from the Lutheran Theological Seminary in Philadelphia, Pennsylvania. In 2012, Walt graduated from Union Presbyterian Seminary in Richmond, Virginia, with a Doctor of Ministry.

Walt lives with his wife in Bonita Springs, Florida. They are the proud parents of two grown sons.

Walt maintains a website filled with devotional materials he has written. *Light From This Hill* is dedicated to shining a little light on your path. If you are interested in finding out more, visit lightfromthishill.com.

Made in the USA
Columbia, SC
01 May 2024

34813189R10113